paradiso

paradiso

recipes & reflections

DENIS COTTER

NINE BEAN ROWS

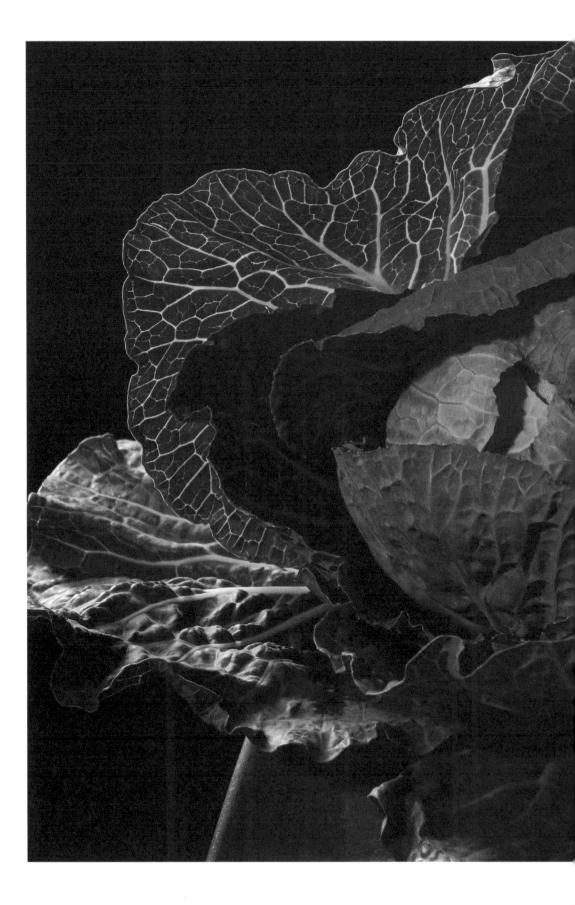

To my grandson, Jimmy Moon, the
embodiment of joy in the present
and optimism for the future.

contents

foreword

I have a deep affection for the food and the philosophy of Paradiso. That affection stems not only from the magnificent food that this restaurant has consistently produced since 1993, but also from my own personal and romantic history.

I met Yvonne in 1996. I was in the process of crashing out of college and rehearsing my first play, *Disco Pigs* by Enda Walsh. Yvonne was a student at the Crawford art school, but more significantly, she was also a waitress at Café Paradiso, as it was then known.

I was subsisting mainly on ham rolls and Beamish. Yvonne was a dedicated vegetarian with an innate understanding of flavour and ingredients that she had refined from watching and working and eating with maestro Denis Cotter.

Many of our early dates were organised by me cycling to Café P and leaving handwritten notes behind the counter there, as I was unsure of her hours. Over the years, it became a place to eat, conspire, plan, recover and celebrate.

Yvonne is now my wife. And while the atmosphere, the warmth and the welcome have never changed in Café P, the food has developed, advanced and evolved to make it one of the greatest places to eat in the world.

Cillian Murphy

introduction

When the idea for this book was first spoken aloud, it was in a half-joking, very casual way. It was only one of a number of ideas rolling around in one of those conversations, the kind that go on for days and weeks in small snippets of chat. It was during the early days of exiting lockdown and there was much to think about. There was also much time to think – a rare luxury in the restaurant business, where all available energy usually goes into keeping the wheels of the present turning and there are few opportunities to stop and look ahead.

The book suggestion came from Meadhbh, the head chef at the time. She said it as though it would be a simple, fun kind of project. I scoffed while mentally noting that that's the attitude that actually gets things done. Still, I didn't think it was something we should spend time on given that we already had four books. Plus the overarching conversation was supposed to be about the future and how we envisaged Paradiso operating in it. My focus was on menu formats, style of cooking, plating and so on.

Then one day I noticed a customer buying a copy of *Paradiso Seasons* after dinner. Not unusual, that – happy customers often want a souvenir of their experience or want to try their hand at replicating some of the dishes at home. But the dishes he ate weren't in that book, I realised, since it was published in 2003, 20 years ago. Suddenly, a new book made sense. The old ones are grand, still full of useful recipes that work and deliver great-tasting food, but as a representation of Paradiso, they are looking back. We needed one that marked our present and pointed forwards.

It didn't look too daunting at first. The information existed and just needed arranging and tidying up. The plan was for Meadhbh to gather and upload recipes from the kitchen that I would then translate into domestic quantities and domestic language. Restaurant kitchen recipes, however, exist in some kind of primitive version of the cloud. One part of a dish is in one chef's notebook and another is in somebody else's, but not the one she uses now, the one before that; it's at home somewhere. Sometimes there are different versions of one dish in everybody's notebook but it's okay because they all remember which version is current and whose notebook it's in. Other parts of a dish might be a mere photograph of wrinkled scraps of paper, sent via WhatsApp by a chef who left two years ago, but that's okay too – everyone instinctively goes to their phones when they need that one. The other thing is the language. Instructions in chef notebooks are literally the definition of notes-to-self. One day I got a recipe for a tricky dessert that was a list of words written in what looked like Arabic journalistic shorthand, with the only discernible instructions being 'make' and '20'.

Another time, unable to find a reliable version of a dish that we hadn't made in a while (a sauce that had been adapted and tweaked often down the years), I remembered that it was descended from something of my own from way back. I took down a copy of the green book, as *Paradiso Seasons* is known in these parts. It wasn't there. Neither was it in *Wild Garlic*. I eventually found it in *The Café Paradiso Cookbook*, aka the yellow book or the 20th-century Paradiso book, as it's now known, having been published in 1999. Reading it, I realised that I needn't have worried about the customer who bought the green book that night. Paradiso is in there all right, even if the exact dishes he ate are not. It's in all the books, of course, the essence of the same food we make today.

Flicking through the old yellow book for the first time in an age, I was reminded again of the strong thread that runs through the decades – how the dishes we make today and the ones we made along the way, no matter how different they look, taste or read on the menu, are all part of one thing that almost has a life of its own. I might then have taken a moment to be grateful that Paradiso is a vibrant, engaged and future-facing thing when it could easily have become a museum by now. I could have given silent thanks to the people who give their youthful energy to keep it that way. I could have, but I don't think I did. I was busy. We had a book to make.

* * *

When Paradiso opened in 1993, it was my hope that it would become a space for me to create a vegetable-based cuisine that could stand with 'normal' restaurants, a place where people went to eat pleasurable, exciting, modern food. I wanted it to eventually lose the word 'vegetarian' and just be a 'restaurant'. I didn't have a clear vision of what the end result would look like and I didn't really know how to go about it other than to open the space and get started. It can't have looked like much of a plan from the outside. Plan B was to emigrate, since that's what everyone else was doing then.

Some research, if I had done any, would have told me that Cork was the right place to start, maybe even the only place in Ireland where it could have worked at the time. There was already a solid food culture here, with plenty of people who were knowledgeable and curious about food on many levels – sourcing, growing, cooking and eating out. And my instinct was right. Having a space within the support and encouragement of that community was liberating and in the years that followed my imagination was allowed to take off on a food trip. Along the way, something that is still identifiably Paradiso came into being.

It was much later, when I was no longer cooking in the kitchen, that I fully understood this. By then, as now, my contribution to the menu and to individual dishes was to sit with the head chef at the long table at the back of the dining room, swapping primitive pencil sketches, writing down groups of words, tasting prototypes and prodding them towards the finish line.

A new dish might start with an old classic and the question: what can we improve? It might start with a series of ingredient words: carrot, sesame, aubergine? Or it might be a whole new idea that the chef wants to try. Even when one of those has reached the stage where it looks good and tastes great, a dish still has to answer the question: is it us, though? Is it Paradiso? Take the pumpkin seed mole that is now a firm favourite in both the kitchen and the dining room. It was created by Eneko, then head chef, with little input from me other than feedback and prompting. The first version was interesting but a bit dull, the fifth one so good we laughed. The differences between each improvement were small and were bridged by a shared understanding of where the dish had to get to, firstly to make it onto the menu and then, in time, hopefully to become part of the repertoire of keeper dishes that come around again and again.

I suppose that's what the thread is made of, the one that connects the present to the past and the future. More than the hard information – the words and numbers in all those notebooks – it's the understanding that is constantly passed along in the kitchen as new ideas mingle with older ones to create a living, evolving repertoire that stays in the place no matter who comes or goes. At any and every point in time, everyone in the kitchen knows what Paradiso food is and how to make it.

This book – the result of all that gathering and translating – could not be called anything other than simply *Paradiso* because that is what it is and what it represents. It is us now. It is our manual for today and, with just a glance at and a nod to the past, it is what the future is always being built on.

Denis Cotter, Cork, 2023

a note on the format

This book is laid out in a way that reflects how dishes are put together in the restaurant kitchen. Behind the part where beautiful plates are put together, there is a whole nuts-and-bolts operation that creates the core elements of dishes, the things that deliver concentrated flavours and textures. These are made separately and have to be put in place before the final assembly of a dish is possible. Even if you cook only a few, or none at all, of the complete plates, I hope you will find some core recipes that will become part of your own store cupboard and that will bring a touch of Paradiso to anything you cook.

In the Plates chapter the recipes have been adapted to individual servings of small plate or starter size, producing dishes that can be served alone or incorporated into menus of a series of courses. There are also a few classic main course-size dishes that are so complete in and of themselves that there was simply no pulling them apart.

These are restaurant dishes and the recipe instructions assume a level of experience in the cook reading them. To reflect the way we work in the restaurant kitchen, the dish recipes include references to smaller recipes in the 'Core Elements' chapter. Following the methods laid out here, the dishes can be made in a calm and organised way by building from the core elements. The best way to do this is to read the plate recipe carefully, work out a plan, make the building blocks ahead of time, then surprise your guests by presenting beautiful, exciting food without breaking a sweat.

All oven temperatures in this book are based on a fan oven. If using a conventional oven, increase the temperature by 20°C. Salt, pepper and oils are not always included in the ingredients list as they are assumed to be staples of every kitchen.

dairy and alternatives

There is always a vegan menu in Paradiso that runs as close as possible to the main one. While we continue to showcase some much-loved local cheeses, we also make some simple non-dairy alternatives that work well as substitutes in many cases. We make a vegan butter too. Those recipes are in the dairy alternatives section of the core elements chapter. There are also some increasingly excellent commercial products available. Whether you make your own or have a favourite brand, throughout this book where a recipe calls for butter it can be read to mean dairy or non-dairy, while for yogurt read dairy, coconut or other plant-based yogurt.

01

IN THE AUTUMN OF 2021, as the restaurants of Ireland moved gingerly back into our dining rooms after a pandemic-induced summer on pavements and patios, Paradiso's menu evolved into a series of smaller sharing plates. In truth, we had wanted to move away from the old à la carte format for a while and the disruptions and adaptions of 2020 and 2021 gave us a window in which to make the leap.

Paradiso has always been about focusing on individual vegetables and then adding elements and textures around, above, below and sometimes inside to create exciting, flavour-driven plates that never lose sight of the character of the vegetable itself. This was always easy to do with traditional starter dishes but harder to maintain on larger main courses, when an otherwise perfect combination required extra elements simply to make the dish more substantial. The new smaller sharing format meant we never had to add bulk to a plate – plus there was the bonus of every diner getting to eat every dish on the menu. A year later, we took the logical next step and put the vegetable-focused dishes back on individual plates in a seasonal six-course menu.

An example of this journey across plating formats is the summer beans with almond satay on page 68, an exciting combination of zingingly fresh, crunchy beans on top of a rich, spicy satay with just a small slice of fried panelle and a scattering of crisped shallots. Originally a popular starter in the old à la carte menu, the dish briefly got a run as a main course with the addition of some sticky black rice and a deep-fried egg. It kind of worked but it was tricky to get the balance right, and for some people – me included – the pleasure of eating it began to fade halfway through. So we liberated the heart of the dish and put it back on the starters side of the menu. That smaller, sharper version of the satay beans is the one that now makes an appearance on our summer menu and in the pages of this book.

With a few exceptions, each of the following recipes makes four portions that work as starters or as part of a multi-dish menu, whether served in courses or as sharing plates.

plates

roasted radishes, cashew cheese, watercress, rhubarb, hazelnut

serves 4

18 radishes

DRESSING:
juice of 1 lemon and zest of ½
100ml olive oil
1 teaspoon sumac

RHUBARB:
80g piece of rhubarb
80g watercress
1 tablespoon sliced fresh basil
1 tablespoon sliced fresh mint

TO FINISH:
cashew cheese (page 202)
2 hazelnuts, lightly toasted

Preheat the oven to 200°C fan.

Set aside two of the radishes. Toss the rest in a little olive oil and salt, then place them on an oven tray and roast in the oven for 15 minutes.

Put the lemon juice and zest, olive oil and sumac in a jar and shake well to emulsify the dressing.

Slice the rhubarb very thinly on a slight diagonal. Thinly slice the two raw radishes. Put the rhubarb and raw radishes in a bowl with the watercress and herbs and add enough of the sumac dressing to coat everything.

To serve, spread some cashew cheese on plates and arrange the roasted radishes on top, cutting any larger ones in half. Place a handful of the salad mix on top and use a fine grater to grate some toasted hazelnuts over each dish.

beetroot risotto, orange, hazelnut crumb, broad beans, Knockalara

serves 4

Our risotto is always made without dairy in the early stage so that it can be finished with olive oil, butter or vegan butter. Where cheese is added to the plated dish, as here with Knockalara sheep's cheese, it can be omitted or replaced with a soft vegan cheese such as the almond feta on page 202.

500g beetroot, roasted and
   peeled
1.5 litres vegetable stock
2 shallots, finely chopped
2 garlic cloves, finely chopped

300g risotto rice, such as
   Carnaroli
125ml red wine
100ml olive oil
50g butter

ORANGE SAUCE:
100g pickled orange (page 179)
100ml olive oil
100ml orange juice

TO FINISH:
2 tablespoons cooked and peeled broad beans
100g Knockalara fresh sheep's cheese, coarsely crumbled
hazelnut crumb (page 170)

GARNISH:
edible flowers

To make the orange sauce, blend the pickled orange, olive oil and orange juice to get a purée with a pouring consistency. Season with salt.

Chop the roasted beetroot and blitz it in a food processor to get a very finely chopped finish.

Keep the stock warm in a pot over a low heat.

Heat a little olive oil in a pan over a medium heat. Add the shallots and garlic and cook for 2 minutes. Add the rice and toast it, stirring often, for 7–8 minutes. Add the red wine and simmer for a few minutes, until it has all been absorbed. Now add a ladle or two of stock and simmer, stirring, until it has been absorbed. Repeat with more stock a number of times, stirring often, until the rice is just tender, approx. 20 minutes. Check the rice grains often in the latter stages.

Stir in the finely chopped beetroot along with the olive oil and butter. Season well with salt and black pepper, then remove from the heat.

Serve the risotto immediately in shallow bowls with some orange sauce spooned around and some broad beans, Knockalara and hazelnut crumb sprinkled over. Garnish with a few edible flowers.

artichoke, carrot, lovage, lemon

serves 4

6 artichokes

CARROT PURÉE:
120g carrots, peeled and chopped
1 small garlic clove
100ml carrot juice
4 teaspoons olive oil
zest and juice of 1 lemon

TO FINISH:
a few lovage leaves
lovage oil (page 195)

To make the carrot purée, bring a pot of salted water to a boil, then add the carrots and cook until soft. Add the garlic clove for 1 minute at the end of the cooking time to blanch it. Strain and put the carrots and garlic clove in a blender with the carrot juice, olive oil and half the lemon juice. Blend to a smooth purée and season with salt. Leave to cool.

Snap off the outer leaves of the artichokes, then peel the base and stem. Trim the stem to 3–4cm in length and cut off the tops of the leaves. Halve the artichokes, check for a choke and remove it if necessary. Drop them into acidulated water (using the remaining lemon juice) as you go to prevent discoloration.

Bring a pot of salted water to a boil. Add the artichokes and boil for 5 minutes to partially cook them. Drain the artichokes and dry on kitchen paper.

Heat a little olive oil in a heavy-based frying pan over a medium-high heat. Add the artichokes and fry for 7–10 minutes, turning occasionally, until tender and coloured. Season with salt.

Fry the lovage leaves in a little olive oil until crisp, then dry them on kitchen paper.

To serve, spoon some of the carrot purée onto plates and place the artichoke halves on top. Dress with a few drops of lovage oil and scatter some fried lovage leaves and lemon zest over everything.

The artichokes should be young and fresh, with little or no hairy choke.

pan-roasted artichokes, nettle broth, lemon arancini, pine nut crumb, smoked tomato purée

serves 4

We alternate the sauce for this dish depending on whether we have wild garlic or nettles. If both are available, we tend to go with nettle.

6–8 small to medium artichokes
lemon juice or vinegar for acidulated water

TO FINISH:
nettle broth or wild garlic broth (pages 190–1)
lemon arancini (page 177)
pine nut crumb (page 171)
smoked tomato purée (page 187)

Snap off the outer leaves of the artichokes, then peel the base and stem of each one. Trim the stem to 3–4cm in length and cut off the tops of the leaves. Halve the artichokes, check for a choke and remove it if necessary. Quarter any larger artichokes. Drop them into acidulated water as you go to prevent discoloration.

Bring a pot of salted water to a boil. Add the artichokes and boil for 5 minutes to partially cook them. Drain the artichokes and dry on kitchen paper.

Heat a little olive oil in a heavy-based pan over a medium-high heat. Add the par-cooked artichokes and fry for 7–10 minutes, turning occasionally, until tender and coloured. Season with salt.

While the artichokes are cooking, warm the broth in a small pan over a low heat.

Heat the oil in a deep-fryer to 180°C. Fry the arancini for 4–5 minutes, until golden brown, then drain them on kitchen paper to dry a little.

To serve, pour some nettle or wild garlic broth into warmed shallow bowls. Add one arancini to each and arrange some pieces of artichoke beside it. Sprinkle over some pine nut crumb and add some blobs of smoked tomato purée.

The artichokes should be young and fresh, with little or no hairy choke.

nettle polenta gnocchi, maple-glazed king oyster, pickled wild garlic buds

serves 4

40g nettle leaves
500ml vegetable stock
100g medium-ground polenta

30g almond feta (page 202)
1 tablespoon nutritional yeast

MAPLE-GLAZED KING OYSTER MUSHROOMS:
4–6 large king oyster
  mushrooms

50ml white wine
25ml maple syrup

TO FINISH:
nettle broth (page 190)
fried nettle leaves

pickled wild garlic buds
  (page 181)

Blanch the nettle leaves in boiling water for 1 minute, then transfer them to cold water. When cooled, squeeze them dry and blitz to a fine pulp in a food processor.

Bring the stock to a boil. Whisk in the polenta, reduce the heat to low and simmer for 10 minutes. Stir in the nettle pulp, almond feta and nutritional yeast and season well with salt.

Place a sheet of parchment on a work surface and spoon some of the polenta mix onto it. Roll and tuck the parchment around the polenta to make a cylinder approx. 2.5cm thick. Set it aside, wrapped tightly in the parchment, to cool and set. Repeat with the rest of the polenta. When cooled, cut the cylinders into pieces 2cm thick.

Cut off the tops of the mushrooms, then cut each top into three slices. Cut the stems into 15mm-thick rounds. Use a knife to score the stem pieces about halfway through in a crisscross pattern.

Heat a little olive oil in a pan over a high heat. Add the mushrooms to the pan with the stem rounds cut side down. Sprinkle with salt and place a light tray on top to press gently on the mushrooms so that they brown evenly. Cook for 5 minutes, then flip each piece over and repeat for the other side, cooking for 3–4 minutes. Check for tenderness with a sharp knife.

Whisk together the white wine and maple syrup, then pour this liquid over the mushrooms in the pan. Let it bubble for a few seconds to coat the mushrooms and deglaze the pan, then transfer the mushrooms to a tray to keep warm in a low oven or to reheat shortly.

To finish, warm the nettle broth gently in a small pan. Fry five pieces of gnocchi per portion on the cut sides in a little olive oil over a high heat, turning once.

To serve, spoon some nettle broth into shallow bowls and arrange the maple-glazed king oysters and the gnocchi on top. Garnish with fried nettle leaves and pickled wild garlic buds.

Irish asparagus ...
for real, like

Local asparagus is a stubborn signifier of its place in the calendar, all the more so because it traditionally arrives in the hungry gap when there is little else around. These days, of course, people only eat nettles for fun, and long may that last. Until fairly recently, however, the arrival of asparagus season was celebrated with imports from France and Spain and, later, England, a celebration compromised by the way that it simultaneously highlighted the absence of a commercial crop of asparagus closer to home.

Now we get all our asparagus (as well as most other vegetables) from Gortnanain, the vegetable farm run by Ultan and Lucy not far outside Cork City. It took a massive amount of work, time, courage and imagination on their part to make that happen, especially as it involved a few false dawns and setbacks over a fair number of years. The asparagus crop is now large enough to supply a number of restaurants in the city and county as well as a few lucky home cooks. Other farmers are growing asparagus too in quantities that can be called commercial crops, to the extent that it can really be said with confidence that, yes, there is such a thing as Irish asparagus.

That statement shows the massive change in accessibility to local produce across the life of Paradiso. Reflecting developments inside Irish restaurant kitchens, there are more people at the growing end too, bringing greatly increased levels of knowledge and expertise in both the field and the kitchen.

Of course, for all its signifying of spring, asparagus is available in supermarkets year round. And it's okay-ish when it's fresh-ish. But Gortnanain asparagus – Irish asparagus – is not just okay tasting; it is amazingly full-flavoured, stridently green and juicy. You can eat it raw and you can grill it hard over high heat to char the skin and bring out the sweetness. Seek some out in the spring. You don't even have to come to Paradiso exclusively to get it any more. That's a good thing. Never thought I'd say that.

asparagus, black garlic, preserved lemon & rosemary purée, viola

serves 4

12 fat asparagus spears
1 lemon
pinch of caster sugar
¼ teaspoon beetroot powder (page 174)
black garlic salt (page 188)

TO FINISH:
black garlic purée (page 188)
preserved lemon and rosemary purée (page 186)

GARNISH:
viola flowers

Snap the ends off the asparagus spears. Slice one spear into thin rounds and place in a bowl. Squeeze some lemon juice over it and add a pinch of salt, a pinch of sugar and the beetroot powder. Stir well and leave to sit for 10 minutes, then drain off the liquid.

Toss the rest of the asparagus in a little olive oil and cook over a high heat on a griddle pan or heavy-based frying pan for 4–5 minutes, until slightly coloured and just tender. Transfer to a bowl and toss with a generous seasoning of the black garlic salt.

To serve, place the seasoned asparagus on plates and add some black garlic purée and preserved lemon and rosemary purée. Scatter the sliced asparagus over the top and finish with some viola flowers.

asparagus, deep-fried egg, coriander, chilli, lime, crisped shallots

serves 4

20g caster sugar
100ml lime juice
zest of 1 lime
1 fresh red chilli, deseeded
1 tablespoon grated fresh ginger
2 teaspoons soy sauce
12 fat asparagus spears

DEEP-FRIED EGG:
4 eggs, at room temperature
1 tablespoon garam masala

TO FINISH:
crisped shallots (page 173)
1 fresh red chilli, deseeded and thinly sliced
coriander leaves

Dissolve the sugar in the lime juice, then blend this with the lime zest, chilli, ginger and soy sauce.

Bring a pot of water to a boil and carefully lower in the eggs. Simmer for 3 minutes 40 seconds, then remove the eggs to a bowl of iced and salted water to stop the cooking. Leave for 20 minutes to cool. Shatter the eggshells by tapping them all over with the back of a spoon, then carefully peel and discard the shell.

Snap the ends off the asparagus spears. Bring a pot of salted water to a boil and drop in the asparagus to blanch for 3–4 minutes, until just tender. Remove and drain on kitchen paper.

At the same time, heat the oil in a deep-fryer to 200°C. Fry the eggs, two at a time, for 1 minute, until they are beginning to colour and crisp. Remove to dry on kitchen paper, then roll the eggs in a light dusting of garam masala.

To serve, place the asparagus spears close together on plates with a deep-fried egg on top. Spoon over some of the dressing followed by a sprinkling of crisped shallots, sliced chilli and coriander leaves.

Accurate timing and some practice are vital to get perfect deep-fried eggs!

asparagus, Hegarty's Cheddar, mustard, hazelnut crumb, fried capers

serves 4

70ml white wine
50ml light vegetable stock
150ml cream
2 teaspoons Dijon mustard (or similar)
60g Hegarty's mature Cheddar, finely grated
12–16 asparagus spears

TO FINISH:
hazelnut crumb (page 170)
fried capers (page 173)

Bring the wine and stock to a boil together in a small pan and simmer to reduce to approximately one-third of the original volume. Add the cream and bring back to a boil, then lower the heat and simmer to reduce to a slightly thickened pouring consistency. Whisk in the mustard and Hegarty's Cheddar. Season with salt and black pepper. Set aside.

Snap the ends off the asparagus spears and discard. Heat a heavy-based frying or griddle pan over a high heat and toss in the asparagus, adding a drizzle of olive oil and a pinch of salt. Cook for 4–5 minutes, tossing often, until the asparagus is seared and just tender.

To serve, arrange the asparagus on small plates. Reheat the mustard cream and pour it over the asparagus. Sprinkle on some hazelnut crumb and some fried capers.

cucumber, peanut rayu, pickled fennel

serves 4–6 as a snack, small plate or starter

2 small cucumbers
black garlic peanut rayu (page 194)
pickled fennel (page 179)

GARNISH:
edible flowers

Using a mandoline or sharp knife, cut the cucumber lengthways into slices approx. 1.5mm thin. Sprinkle the slices with a little salt and leave for 8–10 minutes, then roll the cucumber slices tightly and arrange them on serving plates.

To serve, spoon some rayu over the rolls and drape some pickled fennel on top. Garnish with a few edible flowers.

For best results, you need short, smooth, dark-skinned cucumbers with few or no seeds.

peas, cured egg, basil sablé, pickled fennel, vanilla

serves 4

BASIL SABLÉ:
80g cold butter, diced
45ml basil oil (page 196)

250g plain flour
1 egg

CURED EGG:
200g salt
200g caster sugar

4 egg yolks

PEAS:
420g peas
70ml olive oil
30–40ml water

zest and juice of 1 lemon
80g shallots, finely chopped
12g sugar snaps

TO FINISH:
pickled fennel (page 179)
pea shoots

vanilla oil (page 196)

To make the basil sablé, preheat the oven to 180°C fan. Beat the butter and basil oil together, then stir in the flour. Knead for 2 minutes, then add the egg and knead for 2 minutes more. Roll the dough into a rough rectangle to a thickness of 1cm and place it on a parchment-lined oven tray. Bake for 8–10 minutes, until lightly coloured. Leave it to cool, then cut into very small circles.

To make the cured eggs, combine the salt and sugar in a container. Make four indents and carefully place the egg yolks in them, then cover the yolks with the salt and sugar mix. Chill in the fridge for 1 hour. Remove the yolks with a slotted spoon and carefully rinse them with a little water to clean away the salt and sugar. Put a tablespoon of olive oil on a plate and place the yolks on it.

To prepare the peas, blend 300g of the peas with the olive oil, water and the lemon zest and juice to a smooth purée with the texture of thick pouring cream. Pass through a fine sieve and season with salt.

Sauté the remaining 120g peas with the shallots and sugar snaps in a little olive oil for 2 minutes, then stir in the pea purée and remove the pan from the heat.

To serve, spoon the warm peas into shallow bowls and place a cured egg in each. Add some pickled fennel, the basil sablé biscuits and a few pea shoots, then drizzle some vanilla oil over the dish.

The egg yolk here is cured for just 1 hour so that it remains runny. It is used to thicken and enrich the peas.

chard, tomato, halloumi & lentil timbale, saffron hazelnut butter

serves 4 as a main course

4 large tomatoes
8–10 medium chard leaves
250g halloumi, cut into 6 slices
8 tablespoons braised beluga lentils (page 199)

TO FINISH:
saffron hazelnut butter (page 197)

Preheat the oven to 200°C fan.

Discarding the tops and ends, slice the tomatoes thickly to get three slices from each one. Place the tomato slices on parchment-lined oven trays and drizzle with olive oil and salt. Roast in the oven for 15–20 minutes, until beginning to colour.

Cut the chard leaves near the base and discard the stem. Bring a pot of water to a boil, drop in the leaves and boil them for 4–5 minutes, until tender. Remove the leaves to a bowl of cold water to cool, then dry them on kitchen paper.

Heat a little olive oil in a frying pan over a medium heat. Cut the halloumi slices in half diagonally and fry them for 4–5 minutes, turning once, until coloured on both sides. Transfer the cooked halloumi to a plate lined with kitchen paper.

To assemble the timbales, brush a metal ring with olive oil and line it with chard leaves so that there is enough leaf overhanging to form a closed parcel when filled. Put one or two slices of roast tomato in the bottom and 1 tablespoon of braised beluga lentils on top. Next, add three half-slices of halloumi in a layer, then another tablespoon of lentils and another layer of tomato. Fold over the leaves to make a closed parcel and press down firmly. Repeat to make four timbales.

Place a sheet of parchment paper on top and weigh the timbales down with a plate. Chill in the fridge for at least 30 minutes.

Preheat the oven to 180°C fan.

Place the timbales on a parchment-lined oven tray. Drizzle generously with olive oil and splash a little stock or water on top. Bake in the oven for 12–15 minutes, until the chard is crisping a little on top. Flip the timbales over and leave to rest for a minute or two on the tray.

While the timbales are cooking and resting, warm the saffron butter carefully until it is softened but not melted.

To serve, put a timbale on each plate and spoon some saffron hazelnut butter over to let it melt and make a sauce.

To make the timbales, you will need four metal rings that are 9–10cm diameter.

gazpacho, Macroom buffalo mozzarella, tomato, grilled ciabatta, preserved lemon, dried olives

serves 4

The gazpacho quantities will make enough to serve 6–8, but it's hard to make less. Here it's playing a role closer to that of a generous dressing rather than a soup, so the dish needs just 40ml per portion.

160g large tomatoes, chopped
60g sungold tomatoes, chopped
½ green pepper, deseeded and chopped
¼ cucumber, peeled, deseeded and chopped
20g white bread, torn into pieces
1 garlic clove, chopped
5 teaspoons olive oil
2 teaspoons sherry vinegar

TO FINISH:
1 ciabatta, cut into slices 1cm thick
800g fresh tomatoes
200g Macroom buffalo mozzarella, torn into chunks
preserved lemon and rosemary purée (page 186)
a few small fresh basil leaves
dried olives (page 174)

Put the tomatoes, green pepper, cucumber, bread and garlic in a large bowl. Cover and leave for 1 hour.

Place in a food processor with the olive oil, sherry vinegar and a pinch of salt and blend until smooth. Pass through a sieve and check the seasoning.

Brush the ciabatta with olive oil and toast both sides on a griddle pan, barbecue or heavy-based frying pan.

To serve, ladle some gazpacho into shallow bowls. Slice, halve or chop the remaining tomatoes, depending on size and variety, and arrange them on the gazpacho, adding the mozzarella on top.

Drizzle a little preserved lemon and rosemary purée over the mozzarella, scatter on some basil leaves and sprinkle dried olives over everything. Serve with the grilled bread.

The gazpacho is best eaten on the day it's made.

summer squash flower, pea filling, courgette basil sauce, dried olives

serves 4

160g peas
1 teaspoon finely chopped fresh mint leaves
60g ricotta or cashew cheese (page 202)
4 squash flowers with small squash attached
1 medium courgette
4 fresh basil leaves, thinly sliced
juice of ½ lemon
50g plain flour
25g rice flour
175ml sparkling water

TO FINISH:
courgette basil sauce (page 183)
4 tablespoons peperonata (page 40)
dried olives (page 174)

Blanch the peas by dropping them into boiling water for 30 seconds, then drain and transfer to a bowl of cold water. When cooled, blend 90g of the cooked peas with the mint and coarsely chop the rest.

Stir the blended and chopped peas into the ricotta or cashew cheese, season with salt and pepper and place in a piping bag.

Trim the sides of the squash, then remove the frills at the base of the flower and the pistil from inside. Pipe the pea filling into the flowers until each one is three-quarters full. Twist the top to make a closed parcel.

Just before frying the flowers, use a peeler to slice the courgette into long ribbons and place them in a bowl with the basil and lemon juice. Gently massage and leave to tenderise while you fry the flowers.

Heat the oil in a deep-fryer to 180°C. Whisk together the plain flour, rice flour and sparkling water to make a thin batter. Dredge the flowers in the batter and fry them until crisp, turning once if necessary. Drain on kitchen paper and season lightly with salt.

To serve, put 1 tablespoon of courgette basil sauce and one tablespoon of peperonata on each plate with a fried flower on top and a little gathered bunch of courgette ribbons on the side. Scatter on some dried olives.

grilled peach, cucumber, pickled radish, sheep's milk labneh, mint, watercress, macadamia

serves 4

SHEEP'S MILK LABNEH:
250g sheep's milk yogurt

CUCUMBER PURÉE:
1 medium cucumber, peeled and deseeded
½ ripe avocado
1 spring onion, chopped
1 small garlic clove, chopped
50ml olive oil
juice of ½ lime

GRILLED PEACH SALAD:
1 cucumber
2 peaches
50g watercress
a handful of fresh mint and/or basil leaves
12 macadamia nuts, lightly toasted and halved

TO FINISH:
12 pickled radish slices (page 180)

To make the labneh, strain the yogurt by placing it in muslin or cheesecloth put in a strainer set over a bowl and leaving it in the fridge overnight. Discard the liquid and lightly whisk the remaining labneh.

To make the cucumber purée, blend everything together in a food processor until very smooth. Add a little water if required. Pass the purée through a sieve. Season with salt and chill the purée for at least 1 hour. Before serving, check the seasoning again and add more salt and lime if necessary.

To make the grilled peach salad, use a peeler to get long, wide strips of cucumber. Toss these in a little salt and leave for 10 minutes, then rinse and drain. Cut the peaches in half, remove the stones and cut each half into three wedges. Brush the cut sides lightly with olive oil and grill on a heavy-based frying pan or griddle until blackened.

To finish, spoon some cucumber purée into a shallow bowl. Arrange all the salad ingredients in the centre, garnish with the pickled radish slices and add little spoonfuls of labneh.

smoky peperonata, hazelnut & Templegall gougères, chermoula

serves 4

50ml olive oil
4 red peppers, halved, deseeded and thickly sliced
4 garlic cloves, sliced
1 teaspoon flaky smoked salt
1 tablespoon sherry vinegar
1 teaspoon hot smoked paprika

TO FINISH:
hazelnut and Templegall gougères (page 176)
chermoula (page 194)

GARNISH:
a handful of pea shoots

Heat the olive oil in a heavy-based pan, then add the peppers, garlic and smoked salt. Cover the pan, reduce the heat as low as possible and let the peppers barely stew in the oil for 20 minutes, until they are tender. Season with the sherry vinegar and hot smoked paprika and leave to cool to room temperature.

When cooled, blend half of the peppers to a smooth purée, adding enough of their oily stewing liquid to get the right consistency.

Heat the oil in a deep-fryer to 170°C. Fry the gougères for 4–5 minutes, turning as necessary, until well browned and crisp. Drain on kitchen paper. If you need to do more than one batch, keep the cooked gougères warm in a low oven.

To serve, spread some of the peperonata purée onto plates and place three gougères on top of each portion. Tuck some chunky peperonata around the gougères. Drizzle some chermoula around the dish and garnish generously with pea shoots.

aubergine, black sesame yogurt, zhoug, fried capers

serves 4

2 small aubergines

BLACK SESAME YOGURT:
100g black sesame seeds
100g yogurt
juice of ½ lemon

TO FINISH:
zhoug (page 195)
fried capers (page 173)

GARNISH:
fresh coriander leaves

Preheat the oven to 200°C fan.

Toast the sesame seeds until fragrant. Blend them to a smooth paste in a food processor – this may take 10–15 minutes. Add 2 tablespoons of this black tahini to the yogurt and stir in the lemon juice. Season with salt, taste and add a little more tahini if desired.

Slice the aubergines in half lengthways. Brush both sides with olive oil, season well with salt and place on a parchment-lined oven tray. Roast for 12–15 minutes, until browned and fully cooked.

To serve, spread 1 tablespoon of black sesame yogurt on each plate. Place one aubergine half on top, cut side up. Spread some zhoug on the aubergines and sprinkle over some fried capers and coriander leaves.

Leftover black sesame paste keeps well and can be used like tahini.

Macroom buffalo mozzarella, fennel, strawberry, orange, hazelnut crumb

serves 4

80g strawberries, finely diced
80g fennel, finely diced
zest and juice of 1 lemon
2 tablespoons olive oil, plus extra for drizzling
2 × 150g balls of Macroom buffalo mozzarella

TO FINISH:
1 tablespoon pickled orange (page 179)
hazelnut crumb (page 170)

GARNISH:
small fresh basil leaves
fennel fronds

Gently stir the strawberries, fennel, lemon zest and juice and 1 tablespoon of olive oil together.

Tear the mozzarella balls in half and place each half on a plate, torn side up. Season well with salt and black pepper.

Whisk the pickled orange with the remaining tablespoon of olive oil and a little water to get a thick pouring consistency.

To serve, place the strawberry-fennel mixture in the centre of each portion of mozzarella. Drizzle over a little olive oil and add a little of the orange to the plate. Sprinkle some hazelnut crumb across each portion. Garnish with fresh basil leaves and fennel fronds.

Cáis na Tíre cappelloni, jalapeño, sweetcorn, lime

makes 20 filled pasta (enough for 4 dinner portions or 7–10 starters or small plates)

50g steamed, riced and cooled potato
150g grated Cáis na Tíre sheep's cheese
100g ricotta cheese
350g fresh pasta sheets
1 egg beaten with 2 tablespoons water
2 tablespoons lime butter (page 197)
4 tablespoons jalapeño butter (page 197)

TO FINISH:
sweetcorn espuma (page 192)

GARNISH:
strips of sweetcorn cut from a cooked cob and burned with a blowtorch
sliced rings of jalapeño, burned with a blowtorch
popcorn, coarsely chopped in a food processor
blue cornflowers

Combine the riced potato and cheeses and season with salt and black pepper. Divide into 20 portions and shape each into a semi-sphere. Lay out the pasta sheets and brush with the egg wash. Place the filling portions at the bottom half of the pasta with 5cm of space between. Fold the top half of the pasta over the bottom.

Using your hands, gently shape the pasta around the filling, then use the back of a 3.8cm cutter to press down and create a light indent. Press the edges of the pasta to make a seal and use a 5cm cutter to cut the pasta into the cappelloni 'hat' shape. Store the pasta under a damp cloth on a piece of floured parchment.

Soften the lime butter in a shallow bowl in a warm place. Separately, soften the jalapeño butter until almost melted.

Cook the cappelloni in a pot of boiling salted water for 3 minutes, then drain and toss in the warmed lime butter. Place these in a warm shallow bowl, then dress with some jalapeño butter and spray on the sweetcorn espuma. Garnish with the burnt corn and jalapeño, crushed popcorn and blue cornflowers.

You will need two cutters: one that is 3.8cm in diameter and one that is 5cm.

smoked aubergine, almond feta, tarragon mustard sauce, honeycomb

serves 4

2 slices of bread
2 medium aubergines
120g almond feta (page 202)

TO FINISH:
tarragon mustard sauce (page 183)
1 × 3cm square piece of honeycomb

GARNISH:
a handful of small mustard leaves
coriander oil (page 196)

Cut the bread into rough cubes and toss them in olive oil. Make into croutons either by frying in a pan or toasting in an oven preheated to 180°C fan until crisp.

Cook the whole aubergines for 10–12 minutes, either in the flame of a gas burner or on the griddle of an open fire barbecue. Turn them at least once while they cook to scorch the skin all over. Set aside to cool for 5 minutes, then carefully peel off the skin and discard it.

Slice the smoked aubergines in half lengthways. Brush the slices lightly with olive oil on both sides and cook them again on a heavy-based frying pan over a high heat for 2–3 minutes, until lightly browned.

At the same time, place the almond feta on a tray and brown the top under a hot grill or with a kitchen blowtorch. Break the grilled cheese into chunks.

To serve, spread some tarragon mustard sauce on each plate and put an aubergine slice on top of or beside it, then put some roasted almond feta pieces on the aubergine. Chop the honeycomb and put a piece next to each aubergine slice. Garnish with mustard leaves and a drizzle of coriander oil.

buy from people you like

Even as Paradiso drifts away from dairy we remain devoted to a few small independently made cheeses, and none more so than the fresh sheep's cheese from Knockalara in west County Waterford. Not only because it is a unique cheese – deceptively so, given its simplicity – but also because having it in the house and on the menu is the essence of the old Paradiso maxim of buying from people we like and forming committed relationships with producers. Wolfgang and Agnes make their cheese most months of the year, taking a break in late winter, and when they make it, we use it.

While the focus of our cooking is very much on vegetables, it was through cheese that I first developed contacts with local producers and found a sense of place in the food community. Vegetable farmers came later. Back in the early 1990s, County Cork was almost alone in Ireland in having a resurgent farmhouse cheese industry. While still scrambling around to get decent organic vegetables, I was already buying cheeses directly from the people who made them. Cheeses like Gabriel, Desmond, Durrus and Coolea brought unique character and a local identity to the food I was trying to create. Besides, the cheesemakers were a wonderful, sometimes eccentric, lot and delivery time was always fun. The legendary Bill Hogan of Gabriel cheese fame became a friend through the process of selling me cheese, teaching me how to use it and telling me tall tales. Others came along over time, some of whom are still near constants on the menu: Knockalara, Cratloe Hills, Cáis na Tíre, Templegall, Macroom.

But the role of cheese and our use of dairy has changed. These cheeses are now used only where their character is an integral part of the dish, an example being the recipe that follows as it is as much about the cheese as the aubergine that wraps it. Our in-house cashew cheese makes a decent substitute but it is not the same. Besides signature cheeses, we are always working to take out the casual use of dairy – the cream, butter and milk that can easily be replaced. That approach is reflected in the recipes in this book.

aubergine parcels of Knockalara & spinach, miso gravy, walnut crumb, beluga lentils

serves 4

2 large aubergines
1 small red onion, finely diced
1 garlic clove, finely chopped

400g spinach
180g Knockalara fresh sheep's
    cheese, crumbled

TO FINISH:
braised beluga lentils (page 199)
miso gravy (page 190)
100ml beetroot juice, reduced
    to 2 tablespoons

walnut crumb (page 170)
2 tablespoons boiled and peeled
    broad beans

Preheat the oven to 220°C fan.

Top and tail the aubergines and trim the sides, then cut lengthways into slices 5mm thick. Brush the slices with olive oil on both sides and place on parchment-lined oven trays. Roast in the oven for 10–12 minutes, turning halfway through, until cooked and browned on both sides.

Reduce the oven temperature to 180°C fan.

Heat a little olive oil in a pan and cook the red onion over a medium heat until soft. Add the garlic and cook for 1 minute more. Remove from the heat and set aside.

Blanch the spinach by dropping it into a pot of boiling water briefly, then draining and removing to a bowl of cold water. When cooled, squeeze out the water and finely chop the spinach. Mix the crumbled cheese into the spinach along with the onion and garlic. Season with salt and black pepper.

Lay two slices of roasted aubergine, slightly overlapping lengthways, on a work surface. Put 40g of the spinach and cheese mix in the centre and shape it to make a neat filling 4cm long and to the edges. Fold over the top and bottom of the aubergine slices, turn the parcel over, flatten the top and trim off any excess aubergine slice. Repeat to make eight parcels.

Place the aubergine parcels on a parchment-lined oven tray and cook in the oven for 6–8 minutes to heat through.

Meanwhile, warm the beluga lentils and the miso gravy.

To serve, spoon some beluga lentils onto a plate and drizzle some reduced beetroot juice around the edges. Place two aubergine parcels on the lentils and pour some miso gravy around the lentils. Finish with a sprinkling of walnut crumb and a scattering of broad beans.

You can make these aubergine parcels with other soft cheeses – you can even make them with supermarket feta – and we make a perfectly good version with our homemade cashew cheese on page 202, but Knockalara is the best.

beetroot rasam, cauliflower kofta, coconut, cucumber, radish

serves 4

2 teaspoons chana dal
2 teaspoons toor dal
2 teaspoons coriander seeds
½ teaspoon cumin seeds
½ teaspoon mustard seeds
¼ teaspoon black peppercorns
1 medium red onion, finely diced
1 medium carrot, peeled and finely diced
1 celery stick, finely diced
2 garlic cloves, finely chopped
1 fresh green chilli, finely diced
1 tablespoon finely chopped fresh ginger
1 tablespoon tomato purée
½ teaspoon ground turmeric
800ml vegetable stock or water
500g beetroot, roasted, peeled and diced
1 tablespoon chopped fresh coriander
1 tablespoon tamarind concentrate

TO FINISH:
cauliflower kofta (page 175)
coconut, cucumber and radish raita (page 187)

GARNISH:
a few small fresh mint leaves
edible flowers

Toast the dal, seeds and peppercorns together briefly in a heavy-based pan over a low heat, then grind them to a fine powder.

Heat a little oil in a pot. Add the red onion and sauté for 5 minutes, then add the carrot, celery, garlic, chilli and ginger and sauté for 5 minutes more. Add the tomato purée, turmeric, stock or water and the ground spices. Bring to a boil, then reduce the heat to low and simmer for 20–30 minutes, until everything is tender. Add the roast beetroot, fresh coriander and tamarind concentrate. Blend to a smooth purée, strain through a fine sieve and season with salt.

Heat the oil in a deep-fryer to 180°C. Fry the kofta until browned and crisp, turning once if necessary.

To serve, pour the hot rasam into shallow bowls and add a kofta and a spoon of raita to each. Garnish with fresh mint leaves and a few small edible flowers.

chard, lentil & sticky rice dolma, cashew korma, pistachio dukkah

serves 4

1 teaspoon cumin seeds
200g glutinous black rice
40g beluga lentils
400ml stock
16 medium chard leaves

TO FINISH:
pickled raisins (page 180)
cashew korma (page 182)
pistachio dukkah (page 172)

Preheat the oven to 160°C fan.

Heat 1 tablespoon of olive oil in a pan over a medium heat. Add the cumin seeds and cook for 1 minute. Add the rice and lentils and cook for 3 minutes more. Add the stock, bring to a boil and season with salt.

Transfer to a casserole dish and cover tightly with foil. Bake in the oven for 40 minutes, then remove from the oven, uncover and leave to cool.

Blanch the chard leaves in boiling water, four leaves at a time, for 30 seconds. Remove the leaves and refresh in cold water.

Trim the base of the leaves just above the wide end, removing the thicker lower stem. Flatten the remaining central stem with a rolling pin and lay the leaves on kitchen paper to dry.

Put a chard leaf on a chopping board. Place 1 tablespoon of filling in a line approx. 3cm wide a little up from the wide end. Fold the leaf over it and roll up to halfway. Trim the sides and fold them in to cover the filling. Continue rolling to make a tight parcel. Repeat to fill the other leaves.

Place a large sheet of parchment in a small oven dish, overhanging at the sides. Arrange the filled dolma, tightly packed together, on the parchment. Brush generously with olive oil. Place another sheet of parchment on top and fold over the overlaps to loosely seal.

Bake in the oven for 30 minutes. Leave to cool to room temperature in the parchment.

To serve, place two dolmas on each plate and drizzle a little of the pickled raisin liquid around them. Add some cashew korma. Sprinkle on some pistachio dukkah and scatter pickled raisins on the plate.

is cauliflower having a moment?

Has cauliflower bubbled up through the morass of vegetable ordinariness to become a temporary star? Do vegetables even have moments? Well, yes, if featuring a lot on restaurant menus is a kind of vegetable fame – and especially if playing the star role in the dish for vegetarians. You know the one – celeriac held it for a while and mushrooms have had long periods in the hot seat. The celeriac era was doomed to be short-lived, despite how well it roasts and caramelises when cooked in thick meaty chunks, because the experience of eating a large portion of cranked-up earthy sweetness goes from exciting to overbearing long before the end.

Has cauliflower stepped up because we have all collectively discovered that it roasts really well in big chunks that facilitate knife-and-fork dining, something vegetarians don't get a lot of when eating out? Or because it is equally as comfortable with spices as it is in a soothing blanket of cheese sauce? Maybe, but it has always had these traits and they've been no secret. Once someone put it back on a menu, it was bound to move fast.

Information and trends in food move fast now, ideas are shared openly and a myriad of trends and styles co-exist and cross over. When Paradiso opened, fusion was kicking down the doors of nouvelle cuisine. Fusion came from an idea to present high-quality cooking in deceptively casual settings, coupled with the desire to break away from rigid food cultures that refused to cross borders. Fusion wanted to put the spices and the cheese blanket on the same plate, have some fun and experiment. Nouvelle cuisine looked prim and silly but it was really just an honest attempt to modernise and lighten one of those staid old cultures: the French one. Both styles annoyed some people, and often each other too. Today's fashion for elegant presentations of small, often delicate dishes flavoured with global accents looks like a very happy marriage of the old warring pair. Nouvelle fusion, anyone?

grilled dan dan cauliflower, cashew korma, mustard spinach, pickled raisins

serves 4

1 medium to large cauliflower
dan dan oil (page 195)
pinch of ground nutmeg

MUSTARD SPINACH:
200g spinach
2 tablespoons mustard vinaigrette (page 193)
1 tablespoon coarsely chopped cashews, lightly toasted

TO FINISH:
cashew korma (page 182)
pickled raisins (page 180)

Preheat the oven to 200°C fan. Line an oven dish with parchment paper with an overhang at the sides.

Trim a little from two sides of the cauliflower to get straight edges (keep these trimmings). Slice the head into full cross-section slices about 2.5cm thick. Cut the larger sections into halves or quarters to get one large or two smaller pieces per portion.

Put the cauliflower slices in the lined dish and rub generously and thoroughly with the dan dan oil. Cover the top with more parchment paper and fold over the overhang to make a loosely sealed parcel. Roast in the oven for 20–25 minutes, until just tender but still firm.

Meanwhile, steam approx. 150g of the cauliflower trimmings until soft and blend with 3 tablespoons of olive oil and 1–2 tablespoons of water to get a soft purée. Season with salt and a pinch of nutmeg.

Wilt the spinach in a little olive oil in a pan over a high heat. Remove from the heat and stir in the mustard vinaigrette and chopped cashews.

At the same time, brown the cauliflower slices in a hot frying pan over a high heat.

To serve, place a piece of cauliflower on each plate with a spoonful of cauliflower purée. Drape some mustard spinach over the cauliflower. Spoon some cashew korma onto the plate, then scatter over some pickled raisins and a drizzle of their pickling liquid.

Make the cashew korma and mustard vinaigrette earlier in the day or the day before. The pickled raisins can be made up to a week before and the dan dan oil up to two weeks before.

when the sauce is the dish

Most of the time a dish starts with a vegetable. Then we figure out how to prep it, what shapes to cut it into, whether it should be fried or roasted, steamed or braised. Then we decide how to sauce it and finally we think about what else should go on the plate to show it in its best light. But there are some dishes that start with a sauce because some sauces are so good and so versatile that they remain the focus of a dish no matter what is sitting on top or lurking beneath. They stride across the seasons and often have to be practically dragged, protesting, off the menu to take a little break. With these sauces, we ask not what the vegetable wants but what will serve the sauce.

Romesco is one such sauce. In the version here it sits beneath some romanesco florets, amused at its own word play yet confident in the partnership. Its smoky, lightly spiced combination of roasted peppers and almonds works equally well with sprouting broccoli, artichokes, asparagus, aubergines and grilled leeks or spring onions, the closest we can get to the classic Catalan calçots that are synonymous with romesco in that part of the world.

Another star sauce is the almond satay. Ours is made from a simple whisking together of almond butter and the Paradiso version of dan dan oil that is flavoured with Szechuan peppercorns, chillies, cinnamon and star anise. It is quite addictive and works on any crunchy green vegetable or stirred into noodles. The satay can make an appearance at any time of the year, perhaps peaking in the summer with the fresh long beans from Gortnanain Farm.

But the pumpkin seed chocolate mole is the queen of sauce dishes. Smoky, rich in chocolate and fiery with four or more chilli varieties, the dark mole takes on everything from fried gougères and polenta to roast vegetables like squash in winter and beets in summer. We always add some pickles to cut through but also somehow amplify the heat and richness.

romesco romanesco

serves 4

1 whole bulb of garlic
3 large red peppers
6 medium tomatoes
125ml olive oil
60ml sherry vinegar
2 teaspoons hot smoked paprika
1 teaspoon sweet smoked paprika
150g roasted almonds, coarsely chopped
75g roasted hazelnuts, coarsely chopped
8 fat spring onions
1 small or ½ large romanesco, separated into florets

TO FINISH:
dried olives (page 174)

Preheat the oven to 160°C fan.

Snip the tops off the garlic cloves. Place the bulb on a piece of parchment or foil and drizzle it with olive oil. Seal the garlic into a parcel with the parchment or foil and roast in the oven for 30–40 minutes, until the garlic is very soft. When cooled, squeeze the flesh from the skins.

Blacken the skin of the peppers and tomatoes under a hot grill or over a flame. Place them in a covered bowl to cool. When cool enough to handle, remove and discard the skins and seeds.

Put the peeled vegetables in a sieve to drain for 10 minutes, then into a food processor with the roasted garlic and the olive oil, sherry vinegar and paprikas. Blend to a smooth purée and season with salt. Add the roasted almonds and hazelnuts and pulse a few times to get a textured consistency. Check for salt and sherry vinegar again and add more if required.

Trim away the looser green tops of the spring onions and snip a little off the base.

Heat a heavy-based frying pan or grill pan over a high heat. Lightly oil the spring onions and roast them on the pan, turning once, until blackened on two sides. Remove and set aside.

Brush a little olive oil onto the pan and add the romanesco florets. Season well with salt. Roast for 8–10 minutes, tossing regularly, until well coloured and almost tender throughout. Add a splash of water and cover with a lid to allow the florets to steam for a minute, until fully cooked.

To serve, spread some romesco on plates and arrange the romanesco and spring onions on top. Finish with a sprinkling of dried olives.

pumpkin seed chocolate chilli mole, roast squash, sesame gougères, pickles

makes 8–10 portions of mole

2 cloves
1 × 2cm cinnamon stick
½ star anise
1 teaspoon cumin seeds
80ml olive oil
15g dried ancho chillies
10g dried pasilla chillies
8g dried mulato chillies
8g dried chipotle chillies

1 red onion, finely chopped
½ red pepper, finely chopped
2 garlic cloves, finely chopped
50g fried pumpkin seeds
   (page 172)
1 smoked sun-dried tomato
1 tablespoon sultanas
400ml water
15g chocolate

ROAST SQUASH:
½ small squash, such as Uchiki
   Kuri or Hokaido, unpeeled

juice of ½ lemon

TO FINISH:
sesame gougères (page 176)
pickled red onion (page 178)

pickled jalapeño (page 179)
a few fresh coriander leaves

Grind the cloves, cinnamon, star anise and cumin seeds together.

Warm the olive oil in a heavy-based pan. Lightly fry the dried chillies, being careful not to burn them. Transfer to kitchen paper to drain.

Add the onion, pepper and garlic to the oil. Sauté for 10–12 minutes, until the onion is fully cooked. Add the ground spices and cook for 2 minutes.

Return the chillies to the pan with 40g of the fried pumpkin seeds and the smoked sun-dried tomato, sultanas and water. Bring to a boil, reduce the heat and simmer slowly for 20 minutes.

Transfer to a blender, add the chocolate and blend to a smooth paste. Pass through a fine sieve and season generously with salt.

Preheat the oven to 200°C fan.

Chop the unpeeled squash into wedges. Toss these in a little olive oil and salt and place in an oven dish. Roast in the oven for 20–25 minutes, until tender and lightly coloured. Drizzle with the lemon juice and return to the oven for 5 minutes.

Fry the gougères at 180°C for 4–5 minutes, turning as necessary, until well browned and crisp. Drain on kitchen paper.

Spread some mole on plates. Top with wedges of roast squash and a sesame gougère. Scatter over some pickled red onion and jalapeño along with the remaining fried pumpkin seeds and the coriander leaves.

summer beans, almond satay, coriander panelle, pickled orange, crisped shallots, dillisk powder

serves 4

400g fresh summer beans
3 tablespoons psb dressing (page 193)
8 slices of coriander panelle (page 177)
a squeeze of fresh lemon juice

ALMOND SATAY:
60ml hot water
80g almond butter
1 tablespoon dan dan oil (page 195)

TO FINISH:
pickled orange (page 179)
crisped shallots (page 173)
dillisk powder (see the tip)

To make the almond satay, whisk the hot water into the almond butter to get a thick pouring consistency, then whisk in the dan dan oil and season with salt. Add a little more water if necessary. Leave to cool.

Bring a pot of salted water to a boil, drop in the beans and simmer for 2–3 minutes, until just tender. Transfer the beans to a bowl of cold water to cool, then drain and dry on kitchen paper.

To finish, heat a little oil in a wide pan. Add the blanched beans and toss them over the heat for a few minutes, until heated through. Add the psb dressing and continue to cook for 10–20 seconds to reduce the liquid slightly. Remove from the heat and leave to cool a little.

At the same time, heat the oil in a deep-fryer to 180°C and fry the panelle slices until crisp. Drain on kitchen paper and drizzle with lemon juice.

To serve, place two slices of panelle on each plate and add a pile of warm beans on top. Drizzle a generous dressing of satay around the beans, then add some pickled orange to the plate, some crisped shallots on the beans and a scattering of dillisk powder all around.

Dillisk powder can be bought or made by grinding dried dillisk in a spice grinder.

roast carrots, Macroom buffalo mozzarella, honey, burnt aubergine purée, pickled fennel, ras el hanout crumb

serves 4

4–6 medium carrots
1 tablespoon ras el hanout (page 201)

TO FINISH:
burnt aubergine purée (page 182)
400g Macroom buffalo mozzarella, torn into large pieces
pickled fennel (page 179)
1 tablespoon honey
ras el hanout crumb (page 171)

GARNISH:
fresh fennel fronds

Preheat the oven to 200°C fan.

Peel the carrots and slice them diagonally into long, thick chunks. Cook in boiling salted water for 5 minutes, until almost tender. Drain the carrots and toss them with the ras el hanout, 1 tablespoon of olive oil and some salt. Roast in the oven for 15 minutes, until tender and coloured.

To serve, dot some burnt aubergine purée onto each plate. Arrange the carrots, some large pieces of torn buffalo mozzarella and some pickled fennel on and around the purée. Drizzle a little honey over everything and finish with little mounds of ras el hanout crumb. Garnish with fresh fennel fronds.

smoky za'atar roast squash, lemon tahini, popped barley, mint, pomegranate

serves 4–6

SMOKY ZA'ATAR ROAST SQUASH:
2 tablespoons smoky za'atar (page 200)
2 tablespoons olive oil, plus extra for roasting
1 small or ½ large winter squash, such as Crown Prince, Hokaido or
  Uchiki Kuri

LEMON TAHINI:
2 tablespoons light tahini
1 garlic clove, crushed
juice of ½ lemon
2 tablespoons yogurt

TO FINISH:
popped barley (page 173)
small fresh mint leaves
2 tablespoons pomegranate seeds

Stir 1 tablespoon of the smoky za'atar into the 2 tablespoons olive oil and leave to infuse for at least 1 hour. Strain the oil through a fine sieve.

Preheat the oven to 200°C fan.

Remove the seeds from the squash, then chop it into wedges. Toss the wedges in olive oil and salt and place on a parchment-lined oven tray, spaced apart. Roast for approx. 20 minutes, until lightly browned and tender. Transfer to a bowl and coat with the remaining tablespoon of smoky za'atar, adding a little more olive oil if needed to help it stick.

Make the lemon tahini while the squash is cooking. Whisk some water into the tahini to get a thick pouring texture. Stir in the garlic, lemon juice and yogurt to get a softer mayonnaise-like finish. Season with salt.

To serve, spread some lemon tahini on individual plates or a serving dish. Arrange the squash wedges on top and garnish with the popped barley, mint and pomegranate seeds, finishing with a drizzle of the smoky za'atar oil.

The skin of winter squash is edible and can be left on for dishes like this one, where the squash is roasted in wedges at a high temperature.

togarashi aubergine, sesame greens, maple miso, beetroot, crisped shallots

serves 4

SESAME GREENS:

1 medium pak choi
2 leaves of black or green kale
50g mooli, daikon or kohlrabi
2 tablespoons sliced pickled
  beetroot (page 178)

10g sesame seeds, toasted
3 teaspoons togarashi
  (page 200)
4 tablespoons maple sesame
  ginger dressing (page 193)

AUBERGINES:

2 medium aubergines
100ml vegetable oil
50ml togarashi oil (pages 200–1)

1 tablespoon mirin
1 teaspoon grated fresh ginger

TO FINISH:

maple miso (page 184)
beetroot powder (page 174)

crisped shallots (page 173)

To prepare the sesame greens, slice the pak choi, the kale and the mooli, daikon or kohlrabi into thin strips. Do the same with the pickled beetroot. Place the vegetables in a bowl and add the toasted sesame seeds and 2 teaspoons of the togarashi. Add the maple sesame ginger dressing and mix well.

To prepare the aubergines, preheat the oven to 220°C fan.

Use a peeler to remove four strips of the aubergine skin to create a striped pattern. Cut the aubergines into four slices each, 2cm thick and on a slight diagonal.

Whisk together the vegetable oil, togarashi oil, mirin, ginger and a pinch of salt. Brush the aubergine slices on both sides with this mixture and place them on a parchment-lined oven tray.

Roast the aubergine slices in the oven for 10–12 minutes, until browned on both sides, turning once if necessary. Serve immediately or set aside to be warmed through in the oven just before serving.

To finish, warm the aubergine slices if they have been resting. Place some of the sesame greens on a plate. Top with an aubergine slice, then some more greens, then another aubergine slice. Drizzle some maple miso around the plate, followed by a sprinkling of beetroot powder and the remaining teaspoon of togarashi. Finish with some crisped shallots on top of the aubergine.

pumpkin gnocchi, lemon ginger beurre blanc, burnt leek, hedgehogs

serves 4

½ small Crown Prince pumpkin, deseeded
2 egg yolks

50–60g hard sheep's cheese, finely grated
100–150g plain flour

BURNT LEEK:
1 leek, cut into rounds 2cm thick

HEDGEHOGS:
a handful of hedgehog mushrooms per person

TO FINISH:
lemon ginger beurre blanc (page 192)
basil oil (page 196)

Preheat the oven to 200°C fan.

To make the gnocchi, place the pumpkin, cut side down, on an oven tray lined with parchment paper. Roast in the oven for 30–40 minutes, until tender. If it seems wet, drain any liquid and return the pumpkin to a lower oven heat to dry out further. Leave to cool.

Mash the flesh or pass it through a ricer. Put 500g of the pumpkin mash in a large bowl, then stir in the egg yolks and 50g of the cheese. Add 100g of the flour to make a pliable dough, adding more flour if required. Season with salt and add more cheese to adjust the flavour if you have used additional flour. Roll the dough into long tube shapes approx. 2cm in diameter, then cut these into pieces 2cm long.

Drop the gnocchi into a pot of boiling salted water. When they rise to the surface, cook for 2 minutes more. Remove to a bowl of iced water until cool, then drain and toss in a little olive oil. Set aside.

To make the burnt leeks, heat a cast iron pan until it's searing hot and place the leek rounds on it. Season with salt and place a lid or tray on top to weigh them down. When the leeks are blackened, add a drizzle of olive oil to release them from the pan. Set aside.

To finish, gently warm the lemon ginger beurre blanc in a small pan. Fry the gnocchi in olive oil until coloured. In another pan, fry the mushrooms briefly and season.

To serve, pour some beurre blanc into warmed shallow bowls and arrange the gnocchi, mushrooms and burnt leeks on top. Drizzle over a little basil oil.

This will make a lot of gnocchi, but it's best to make gnocchi in larger batches. You can freeze the excess on trays sprinkled with rice flour. When frozen, transfer to sealed containers. Bring back to room temperature before cooking.

walnut tortellini, spiced aubergine, miso, orange

makes 24–28 tortellini (serves 4 as a main dish or 12 small plates or starters)

SPICED AUBERGINE:

2 aubergines, chopped into
1cm dice
1 red onion, finely chopped
4 garlic cloves, finely chopped
8 dried bird's eye chillies, ground

1 tablespoon fresh thyme leaves
1 tablespoon coriander seeds,
ground
100ml red wine
250ml passata

WALNUT TORTELLINI:

200g cooked cannellini beans
150g walnuts
50ml olive oil

2 teaspoons tamari
350g fresh pasta sheets

TO FINISH:

orange butter (page 196)
aubergine miso purée (page 184)

Preheat the oven to 200°C fan.

Place the orange butter in a shallow dish in a warm place to soften.

Toss the diced aubergines in olive oil and roast in the oven for 15–20 minutes, until coloured and tender.

Sauté the red onion in a little olive oil over a medium heat for 7–8 minutes. Add the garlic, ground chillies, thyme and ground coriander and cook for 3 minutes more. Add the red wine and simmer for 2 minutes, then add the passata. Bring to a boil, then reduce the heat to low and simmer for 20–25 minutes. Blend in a food processor, then return the sauce to the pot, stir in the roasted aubergine cubes and season with salt.

To make the pasta filling, put the cannellini beans, walnuts, olive oil and tamari in a food processor and blend to a slightly coarse purée.

Lay out the pasta sheet and cut out 8cm circles. Place a generous teaspoon of filling in each circle, then brush the edges with water and fold over the pasta to make a half-moon-shaped parcel. Twist the pointed ends to meet and press them together to make a tortellini. Store the filled pasta under a damp cloth on a piece of floured parchment.

Cook the tortellini in a pot of boiling salted water for 3–4 minutes, then drain and toss in the softened orange butter.

To serve, spread some aubergine miso purée onto plates and place the orange-buttered tortellini on top. Spoon some spiced aubergine onto and around the pasta.

# of cake, jam and men

Ah, the good old couscous cake. This decades-long stalwart of the dinner menu made its publishing debut in *Paradiso Seasons* in 2003. Much later, during the lockdowns of 2020 and 2021, the couscous cake was the most-ordered dish on our 'finish at home' meal kit service. Those cakes were sent out shaped and ready to fry, wrapped tightly in a 'metal' ring made from tinfoil using a cardboard template. Sam made every single one of those rings – hundreds of them – as nobody else seemed able to master the time-consuming technique. Strange, that.

The other strange thing about the couscous cake's success and longevity is that very early in its career it somehow became the 'safe' dish on the menu, the one chosen by people who were a bit nervous going to a vegetarian restaurant. This phenomenon is almost gone now, but for a long time it was obvious that some people were coming with some apprehension and doubts about whether they would enjoy the food or feel satisfied afterwards. We're talking about men here, obviously.

I did a survey once back then, the result of which was that the percentage of men in the dining room went from 20% on Tuesdays to 50% on Saturdays. The conclusion was that men were left behind during the week and 'brought' on the weekend. Anyway, the men took to ordering the couscous cake as the safe and solid option, and it got locked into the menu to play that role. Now I completely understand why the dish is so satisfying. It has a wonderful combination of flavour, texture, richness and greenery, with gentle and warm spicing. What seems strange is how the combination of words on the menu came to signify safety and comfort to the cautious: *feta, pistachio, couscous, cake, smoky greens, lemony chickpeas, yogurt, date jam*. I think it must be the words *cake* and *jam*.

As I write, the couscous cake hasn't found a place on the new menu format. We haven't given up on it, however. It's sitting on the subs bench, togged out and warmed up.

feta & pistachio couscous cake, smoky greens, lemony chickpeas, date jam

makes 4

2 medium red onions, finely chopped
2 garlic cloves, finely chopped
½ tablespoon whole cumin seeds, lightly toasted
1 tablespoon couscous spice (page 200)

220ml water or vegetable stock
250g couscous
100g fresh coriander, chopped
80g pistachios, toasted and coarsely chopped
2 eggs, beaten
300g feta cheese, crumbled

LEMONY CHICKPEAS:
1 × 400g tin of chickpeas, including the water
1 tablespoon preserved lemon purée (page 186)

SMOKY GREENS:
½ red onion, thinly sliced
½ red pepper, thinly sliced

2 handfuls of chopped kale
1 teaspoon hot smoked paprika

TO FINISH:
coriander yogurt (page 187)
zhoug (page 195)

date jam (page 189)

Sauté the red onions in olive oil over a medium heat for 5 minutes, then add the garlic and cook for 2–3 minutes. Add the cumin and cook for 1 minute. Add the spice mix and a splash of water or stock to deglaze, then add the rest of the liquid and warm it to 50°C–60°C.

Put the couscous in a large bowl and stir in the onion mix. Cover and leave for 15–20 minutes, then fluff up the couscous with a fork. Stir in the coriander, pistachios and beaten eggs, then fold in the feta.

Warm a wide, heavy-based frying pan over a medium heat. Brush four metal rings with oil and fill with the couscous mix. Cook in the pan for 8–10 minutes, until crisp and browned on each side.

Bring the chickpeas, their water and the lemon purée to a boil in a small pan. Simmer for 5 minutes to thicken slightly. Season with salt.

In another pan, heat 2 tablespoons of olive oil over a high heat. Add the red onion and pepper and cook, stirring, until beginning to brown. Add the kale and continue to cook over a high heat, stirring, until it has wilted. Add a splash of water and cook for 2 minutes, until the greens are tender. Add the paprika and season with salt.

To serve, place some greens on each plate and put a cake on top. Add chickpeas, coriander yogurt and zhoug. Add a spoonful of date jam on each cake.

You will need four metal rings 9–10cm in diameter and 3cm high.

paradiso

chilli-glazed tofu, coconut tamarind broth, pak choi, crisped vermicelli

serves 2 as a main course with rice or noodles or serves 4 as a starter or small plate

100g sambal oelek
35g caster sugar
juice of ½ lemon
50ml tamari
50ml water
400g firm tofu, cut into 8 slices
coconut tamarind broth (page 191)
2 small heads of pak choi, halved or thickly sliced

TO FINISH:
crisped vermicelli (page 173)

Whisk together the sambal oelek, sugar, lemon juice, tamari and water. Place the tofu slices in the marinade for 10 minutes prior to frying.

Heat a little oil in a wide, heavy-based frying pan. Fry the tofu slices over a high heat, turning once, until well browned on both sides.

Spoon over some of the marinade (2 teaspoons per slice) and continue cooking, swirling the pan occasionally, until the marinade has coated and glazed the tofu.

At the same time, heat the coconut tamarind broth in a separate shallow pot. Add the pak choi and cook for 2 minutes.

To plate, place some pak choi in shallow bowls and pour over some of the coconut tamarind broth. Arrange the glazed tofu slices on the pak choi and top with crisped vermicelli.

the night of the turnip

One quietish evening in the Paradiso kitchen, I was feeling something that I've often described in the telling of this as boredom. But I think it should properly be identified as a need to do something creative.

I hadn't had a great idea in a while. I was staring at a turnip. A big, ugly, misshapen lump of a thing, almost a sphere but not quite, like a planet that had been crashed into and left dented and pockmarked. I cut off the top and bottom, trimmed the sides, tidied up the edges and suddenly found that I was looking at a cube. A perfect, creamy yellow cube that seemed as full of potential as the turnip had seemed uninspiring.

Next I cut the cube into thin slices like lasagne sheets, stacked them up and stared some more. Eventually I braised the slices in wine and butter until they were succulent and richly flavoured. The turnip chestnut galette was born that night, though it took a couple days to work out the filling and settle on a sauce. From the scraps we made ravioli filled with turnip and smoked cheese, a dish that stayed on the menu for a while but never became locked into the repertoire the way the galette did.

I went on a bit of a solo run then, and for a while ideas came quickly and developed easily into keeper dishes. Looking back from quite a distance it seems now that a lot of that kind of creative work was done in short bursts like the one that began with the turnip, and maybe even that the best of it was in a shorter period than it felt like at the time. That seems common enough in other fields, music especially, where a core body of work is often created in a few short years, even if this isn't clear until much later.

Luckily, Paradiso hasn't depended solely on me for creative input for some years. Since Eneko Lopez first became head chef, followed by Meadhbh Halton and then Miguel Frutos, it has been a collaborative effort in which my job is mostly to help guide their new ideas and techniques into something that fits the ever-evolving but still recognisably Paradiso repertoire.

braised turnip, chestnut & portobello galette, beetroot port gravy

serves 4 as a main course

4 large portobello mushrooms
100g cooked chestnuts
100g cream cheese or cashew
  cheese (page 202)
2 large turnips

50g butter, plus extra melted
  butter for brushing
250ml water or vegetable stock
100ml white wine
50ml maple syrup

TO FINISH:
beetroot port gravy (page 190)

Preheat the oven to 200°C fan.

Brush the mushrooms with melted butter or olive oil and season with salt, then roast in the oven for 10–12 minutes, until well done. Drain any excess liquid and pulse the mushrooms with the chestnuts in a food processor to a coarse purée. When cool, stir in the cream cheese or cashew cheese.

Lower the oven temperature to 160°C fan.

Peel the turnips and trim to a square or rectangular block. Cut into square slices measuring 7–8cm on the sides and 3mm thick – you want to have four slices per galette, so you need 16 slices in total. Boil in salted water for 7 minutes, then transfer the slices to a parchment-lined shallow oven dish, laying the slices flat but slightly overlapping. You may need two oven dishes for this stage.

Melt the butter, water or stock, wine and maple syrup together and pour this over the turnip slices. Cover loosely with parchment paper and cook in the oven for 40 minutes or more, until the turnips are soft enough to yield easily to a table knife. When fully cooked, remove the slices from the liquid and set aside.

To finish the galettes, raise the oven temperature to 200°C fan.

Place the four slices of turnip on a parchment-lined oven tray and cover with some of the mushroom and chestnut purée, leaving a narrow edge clear on all sides. Repeat until each galette has four turnip layers and three layers of the mushroom and chestnut purée. Press firmly to get a flat, even top. Brush the tops with melted butter, then place the galettes in the oven to heat through for 7–10 minutes.

To serve, place a galette on each of four plates and pour a generous pool of beetroot port gravy around.

Make the beetroot port gravy earlier in the day.

Serve with a potato side, such as the horseradish mash on page 124, and some simply cooked sprouts.

scorzonera fritters, hazelnut rayu sprout tops, miso mayo, pickled plum

serves 4

6 scorzonera roots
lemon juice or vinegar for acidulated water
200g panko breadcrumbs
100g plain flour
100ml water

HAZELNUT RAYU SPROUT TOPS:
1 head of sprout tops, sliced into ribbons
4 teaspoons hazelnut rayu (page 194)

TO FINISH:
miso mayo (page 185)
pickled plum (page 181)

GARNISH:
½ teaspoon black sesame seeds
½ teaspoon white sesame seeds

Wash and peel the scorzonera, putting the peeled ones in acidulated water to avoid discolouring.

Bring a pot of generously salted water to a boil and cook the scorzonera in it for 8–10 minutes, until just tender. Check often, as pieces can cook at different rates. Remove the cooked pieces to a bowl of cold water, then to a tray lined with kitchen paper to dry.

Blitz the panko crumbs briefly in a food processor to get a finer crumb.

Whisk together the flour and water and season with salt. Cut the scorzonera into angled pieces approx. 5–6cm long. Coat these in the flour and water paste, then in the panko crumbs.

Heat the oil in a deep-fryer to 180°C. Fry the fritters until golden and crisp. Remove to a paper-lined tray to drain off excess oil and season lightly with salt.

While the fritters are cooking, heat some olive oil in a pan over a medium heat. Add the sliced sprout tops and sauté until tender, adding a splash of water once or twice. Finish by adding 1 teaspoon of hazelnut rayu per portion, then remove the pan from the heat.

To serve, place some rayu-dressed greens on a plate and arrange the scorzonera fritters on top. Dot some miso mayo around and finish with some pieces of pickled plum and pickling juice. Garnish with a sprinkling of black and white sesame seeds.

Cavolo nero or a dark green cabbage can be used instead of sprout tops.

tofu, black garlic peanut rayu, pickled red onion, chermoula, crisped shallots

serves 4

500g silken tofu
4 tablespoons black garlic peanut rayu (page 194)
1 tablespoon chermoula (page 194)
pickled red onion (page 178)
crisped shallots (page 173)
fresh coriander leaves

Cut the tofu into four blocks and place them on small plates. Warm the rayu gently to approx. 75°C – do not boil it.

To serve, pour 1 tablespoon of the warmed rayu over each portion of tofu. Drizzle some chermoula around the plate and garnish with the pickled onion, crisped shallots and fresh coriander leaves.

parsnip gnocchi, sprout tops, roast pear, walnut miso sauce, sage, chilli

makes 28–30 gnocchi (serves 4–5 as a main dish or 7–10 small plates)

800g raw parsnips, peeled, cored
   and chopped
2 egg yolks
20g hard sheep's cheese, such as
   Cratloe Hills
pinch of grated nutmeg

150–180g plain flour
1 firm pear
a handful of sprout top leaves,
   thinly sliced
12 fresh sage leaves

TO FINISH:
sage and chilli butter (page 196)
walnut miso sauce (page 191)

Preheat the oven to 160°C fan.

Steam the parsnips for 8–10 minutes, until soft. Transfer to an oven tray and place in the oven for 20 minutes to dry a little. Gently mash the cooked parsnips or pass through a ricer, then leave to cool.

Weigh approx. 375g of the cooled parsnip into a bowl. Add the egg yolks, hard cheese, nutmeg and 150g of flour. Season well with salt. Fold together to get a pliable dough, adding a little more flour if necessary. Roll the dough into cylinders approx. 25mm thick, then cut into 20mm pieces – you should get 28–30 pieces of gnocchi.

Bring a pot of water to a boil and drop in the gnocchi in batches, cooking each batch for 4–5 minutes, until they float to the top. Scoop out the cooked gnocchi and drop them into cold water to cool quickly. When they are all done, drain them and set aside.

Meanwhile, increase the oven temperature to 200°C fan. Quarter the pear and remove the core. Halve each quarter again lengthways, toss these wedges in a little olive oil and roast them in the oven for 20 minutes.

Heat a little olive oil in a pan over a medium-high heat. Add the sage leaves and fry for 30 seconds or so, until crisp. Transfer to a plate lined with kitchen paper to dry.

To finish, fry the sprout tops in a little olive oil, stirring often, for 5–7 minutes, until tender. Season with salt.

In another pan, fry the gnocchi in olive oil until browned, then remove from the heat and add 1 tablespoon of sage and chilli butter for each portion.

Warm the walnut miso sauce gently in a small pan, adding a little water if it's too thick.

To serve, spoon some warm walnut miso sauce onto plates and place the parsnip gnocchi on top. Add the fried sprout tops and roasted pear slices, then spoon some of the melted sage and chilli butter from the pan over everything. Garnish with the fried sage leaves.

gingered adzuki bean wontons, strange sauce mayo

makes enough for 30 wontons, perfect for a party snack

Commercial wonton wrappers are generally excellent but usually contain egg, so here's a simple eggless recipe to make your own if that's your inclination.

120g adzuki beans, cooked (to yield 300g)
1 red onion, finely chopped
2 tablespoons grated fresh ginger

1 tablespoon coriander seeds, ground
1 star anise, ground
4 teaspoons soy sauce
1 tablespoon tomato purée

WONTON WRAPPERS:
200g plain or strong white flour
100ml warm water

½ teaspoon salt

STRANGE SAUCE MAYO:
2 tablespoons vegan mayo
1 tablespoon strange sauce (page 184)

GARNISH:
black and white sesame seeds

To make your own wonton wrappers, make a dough with the flour, water and salt. Knead briefly until it's smooth and elastic, then leave to rest for 30 minutes.

Coarsely mash the cooked adzuki beans and set aside.

Heat a little vegetable oil in a heavy-based pan over a medium heat. Add the onion and fry for 1 minute, then add the ginger and ground spices and cook for 1 minute more. Add the adzuki bean mash, soy sauce and tomato purée and cook for 5 minutes, stirring constantly. Leave to cool.

Roll the dough as thinly as possible and cut into 8–9cm squares. Place some of these wonton wrappers on a work surface. Put 1 teaspoon of filling in the centre of each wonton, moisten the edges with water and fold up to form a filled triangle. Moisten two corners and fold again to make a standing triangle. Repeat with the remaining wrappers and filling.

Make a sauce by stirring the mayo and strange sauce together.

Heat the oil in a deep-fryer to 180°C. Fry the wontons for 2–3 minutes, until browned and crisp. Drain briefly on kitchen paper.

Serve warm with the strange sauce as a sauce or a dip. Scatter over some black and white sesame seeds to garnish.

The filling will keep for three or four days.

farmers, cooks and gnarly tubers

Most vegetables have a season that begins slowly, peaks with a mountain of bounty and fades out slowly. Usually there is something new coming in as the old fades out. Very occasionally, that end to a long season is like a song you wish would just stop – you wind up pulling the needle off the record. We had that 'Hey Jude' experience with sunchokes, the plant so in love with itself it can't stop giving. We haven't used it for a couple of years simply because life is easier without it rather than committing to its seemingly never-ending season. The farmer was happy to take a break too. If he hadn't wanted to, we might have had to carry on. That's all part of the balance between farmer and cook.

Mashua, a tuber of South American origin, is a recent example of a vegetable that arrived in the Paradiso kitchen because Gortnanain Farm took to growing it and liked doing so, meaning we had to figure out a use for it. That's okay; other times we make them grow something we want. Well, we try to, anyway.

With a new vegetable it can take two years to work out that balance, and more like four before it feels comfortable. Some don't make it past year one, while others become staples. Mashua had a brilliant first year. It grew well for the farmer and the kitchen figured out ways to work with it. Customers loved the novelty and appearance of it, and anyway, that ginger and lime sauce would make anything taste great. But some people didn't like its cooked texture, signalling that mashua might have a Marmite-esque love/hate quality about it.

The crop was equally successful the second time round, but with the novelty gone, both the kitchen and dining room were just a tiny bit less enthusiastic. Year three's crop failed completely for a reason the farmer assures us is a one-off. The kitchen, slightly discombobulated at losing a key winter ingredient, was also quietly relieved. Will mashua be back? Will we go back to loving it? Years four to six will tell. Such is the cycle of a farm–kitchen relationship.

roast mashua, ginger lime curry, mango mashua salsa, cheese curds, broad beans

serves 4

ROAST MASHUA:
8 mashua, washed

MANGO MASHUA SALSA:
1 mashua, washed
¼ mango, peeled
½ fresh red chilli, deseeded

juice of ½ lime
½ teaspoon brown sugar

CHEESE CURDS:
3g vegetarian rennet
50ml water
1.5 litres milk

100ml kefir
100ml cream

TO FINISH:
ginger lime curry (page 192)
2 tablespoons boiled and peeled broad beans

To make the cheese curds, stir the rennet into the water. Put the milk and kefir into a sterilised pot and bring up to 29°C, then remove from the heat. Add the water and rennet mix and stir briefly to combine, then stand the stirring spoon straight up in the pot to stop the liquid movement. Leave it to rest, covered, in a warm spot for 15 minutes.

Cut across the mix with a palette knife a few times, then turn the pot 90 degrees and repeat. Rest the mix for a further 45 minutes, then strain through cheesecloth. Leave it straining overnight in the fridge.

The next day, remove the cheese from the cloth, place it in a bowl and break it apart into soft lumps of curd with a wire whisk. Stir in the cream and season with salt to taste.

To roast the mashua, preheat the oven to 200°C fan.

In an oven dish, toss the mashua in olive oil and salt and roast in the oven for 20–30 minutes, until soft. Turn each mashua after 10 minutes and continue to check them often after that. They will all cook at different rates and can quickly become too soft, so remove each one as it is cooked.

While the mashua are cooking, peel and finely dice the remaining mashua. Dice the mango and red chilli to the same size and stir the three together with the lime juice and brown sugar to make a salsa.

To finish, warm the ginger lime curry and spoon some onto plates. Place two roasted mashua on top and scatter over some cheese curds, salsa and broad beans.

The cheese curds makes 500g (15–25 portions to scatter over a small dish) and will keep for three to four days in the fridge.

celeriac terrine, apple, cabbage, fennel

makes 6–8 portions

CELERIAC TERRINE:
1 large celeriac, approx. 1.2kg to give 850g net weight
250g salted butter
200g Crozier Blue cheese

APPLE, CABBAGE, FENNEL:
1 small red apple
1 small wedge of red cabbage
pickled fennel (page 179)

TO FINISH:
red cabbage sauce (page 183)
1 braised fennel (page 112)

GARNISH:
fresh fennel fronds

Preheat the oven to 160°C fan.

Peel the celeriac and cut it in quarters vertically. Slice the quarters into pieces approx. 3mm thick using a mandoline.

Melt the butter and whisk in the blue cheese, then fold this into the celeriac slices. Season with salt and pepper.

Line a standard loaf tin (22cm × 12cm) and layer in the celeriac mix. Cover with parchment and cook in the oven for 1 hour. Test with a sharp knife to check that the terrine is tender all the way through – cook for a further 20–30 minutes if necessary.

Remove the terrine from the oven and place a weight on top to press it while it cools for a few hours or overnight.

When cooled, turn the terrine out onto a chopping board and slice into portions. Warm these through in a moderate oven for 6–8 minutes before serving warm.

Warm the red cabbage sauce gently to room temperature.

Blend the braised fennel to a purée, adding a little water or olive oil as necessary.

Slice the apple and red cabbage into matchsticks. Combine equal quantities of apple, red cabbage and pickled fennel.

To serve, plate a slice of warm terrine with a spoonful of the fennel purée, a drizzle of red cabbage sauce and a small pile of apple, cabbage and fennel. Garnish with fresh fennel fronds.

This quantity fills a standard loaf tin (22cm × 12cm).

napa cabbage, lentils, fennel, capers, smoked tomato

serves 4

100ml olive oil
2 garlic cloves, sliced
75ml white wine
½ napa cabbage, cut lengthways
20g beluga lentils
fennel caper salsa (page 188)

TO FINISH:
smoked tomato purée (page 187)

Preheat the oven to 200°C fan.

Heat 25ml of the olive oil in a small pan. Add the garlic and gently sauté for 2–3 minutes, until just beginning to turn golden. Add the wine and keep warm over a low heat.

Slice the cabbage half into four long wedges. Heat a little more oil in a wide pan and fry the cabbage over a high heat, turning once to brown both of the cut sides. Transfer the cabbage wedges to an oven tray lined with enough parchment to fold over.

Add the remaining olive oil to the wine and garlic. Heat it through and pour it over the cabbage. Season with salt and fold over the parchment to make a seal. Braise in the oven for 25–30 minutes, until tender.

Meanwhile, cook the beluga lentils in a pot of boiling water for approx. 20 minutes, until just tender. Drain and cool in a sieve, then stir the cooked lentils into the fennel caper salsa. Check the seasoning and add more salt if required.

To serve, place the cabbage on small individual plates or one large serving plate and spoon some of the lentils and salsa over each wedge. Dot some smoked tomato purée on the plate.

The recipe needs just half a napa cabbage for four portions as a side or sharing dish. If you want to use the whole cabbage, double the rest of the ingredients.

lime-grilled halloumi, spiced carrot purée, pistachio dukkah, beluga lentils, beetroot harissa

serves 4

250g halloumi
1 lime

TO FINISH:
braised beluga lentils (page 199)
spiced carrot purée (page 184), at room temperature
beetroot harissa (page 187)
pistachio dukkah (page 172)

Cut the halloumi into slices 1cm thick, then cut each slice in half again.

Heat a little olive oil in a frying pan over a high heat. Add the halloumi slices and cook for a few minutes, until browned and crisp on both sides. Squeeze the juice of the lime over the halloumi in the pan, then remove the pan from the heat.

At the same time, warm the beluga lentils.

To serve, spread the spiced carrot purée and beetroot harissa on plates and spoon some beluga lentils on top. Arrange the halloumi on top, then sprinkle over some pistachio dukkah.

We mostly use halloumi made by Macroom Buffalo Farm in County Cork. Alternatively, traditional halloumi from Cyprus or some of the excellent vegan halloumi brands now available.

vermicelli, king oyster mushrooms, pickled cabbage, fried peanuts

serves 4–6

HOT PEPPER OIL:
10 garlic cloves, thinly sliced
200ml extra virgin olive oil

1 teaspoon Korean hot
  pepper flakes

MUSHROOMS:
4 king oyster mushrooms

DRESSING:
50ml rice vinegar
25ml tamari
10g finely chopped fresh ginger

2 teaspoons Shaoxing
  cooking wine

NOODLES:
400g thin vermicelli rice noodles
1 tablespoon toasted sesame oil
20 fresh mint leaves, thinly
  sliced

20 fresh coriander leaves,
  thinly sliced
2 spring onions, thinly sliced
fried peanuts (page 172)

TO FINISH:
pickled red cabbage (page 178)

GARNISH:
edible flowers

Put the garlic in a pot with the olive oil and gently warm it over a low heat. When the garlic is beginning to colour, sieve it out and leave on kitchen paper to dry. Remove half of the oil (leaving the rest of the oil in the pot), add the Korean hot pepper flakes to it and leave to cool to be used in the dressing.

Cut the tops off the mushrooms and shred the stems with a fork. Slice the tops thinly. Increase the heat under the pot and add the mushrooms, frying them until crisp. Remove from the oil and leave on kitchen paper to dry.

Make the dressing by whisking together the reserved 100ml of spiced olive oil and the rice vinegar, tamari, chopped fresh ginger and Shaoxing cooking wine.

Cook the vermicelli noodles by covering them with boiling water for 5 minutes. Strain and rinse with cold water until cool, then toss with the sesame oil in a large bowl. Add the herbs and spring onions along with the fried peanuts, garlic, mushrooms and the dressing.

To serve, plate portions of the salad with some pickled red cabbage alongside. Garnish with a few edible flowers.

braised fennel, chilli, coriander, lime

serves 4

2 large fennel bulbs
150ml vegetable stock or water
100ml white wine
1 tablespoon maple syrup
2 star anise
zest and juice of 1 lime
1 fresh red chilli, halved, deseeded and sliced
a few fresh coriander leaves

Preheat the oven to 180°C fan.

Trim the tops and bases of the fennel bulbs. Cut each bulb into four or six pieces lengthways, depending on the thickness of the bulb.

Heat some olive oil in a wide pan over a medium-high heat. Add the fennel and fry until browned on both cut sides. Pour in the stock or water, wine, maple syrup, add the star anise and season with salt, then bring the liquids to a boil.

Transfer the fennel and the pan liquid to an oven dish, cover loosely with parchment and braise in the oven for 30–40 minutes, until tender. Transfer the braised fennel to a serving dish, discarding most of the remaining braising liquid.

To serve, pour the lime juice over the fennel and sprinkle on the lime zest, then scatter over the sliced chilli and coriander leaves.

flowering sprouts, chilli, hazelnut rayu

serves 4

Flowering sprouts (aka frivole) are a recently introduced sprouting brassica that looks like a Brussels sprout plant and produces loose sprouting florets instead of tight heads. This recipe works well with all the dark greens, sprouting or otherwise, new or ancient.

a handful of flowering sprouts per portion
1 fresh red chilli, deseeded and sliced
hazelnut rayu (page 194)

Heat some olive oil in a pan over a medium-high heat. Add the sprouts and cook for a few minutes, until tender. Add the sliced chilli just before the end of the cooking time. Add 1 tablespoon of hazelnut rayu per portion and take the pan off the heat. Leave for 1 minute before serving.

To serve, transfer the greens to a plate and spoon over the rayu and pan juices.

02

THERE IS ALMOST ALWAYS a potato dish on the menu. I say 'almost' for a couple of reasons. Firstly, I can't predict the future, even though the business of running a restaurant involves a certain amount of gazing into it and acting as though you can indeed see around corners. There are potatoes on the menu now as I write, and that's as far as I'm willing to commit. Secondly, it's happened before. There was that time my mother brought some old friends of hers to the restaurant, people I also knew from decades of Sunday afternoon visits, funerals and the like. Confused by the words on the menu, and even more so by the ones not on it, one of them bypassed the dining room staff and came up to the counter of the open kitchen, where I was busy putting finishing touches to plates.

'Denis,' he said, 'there are no spuds?!' It was part question and part statement of disbelief. I confirmed that was the case, adding that there were none in the house so I couldn't even do anything about it. 'And no apple tart!' he added in a voice that was almost pleading for some sanity to be restored to the situation. No apple tart either, I had to confess. He went back to his table, shaking his head. My mind has since blanked what he ate or if he liked any of it at all, but I do remember that soon after, potatoes went back on the menu. Perhaps that was when the Paradiso fries were invented. Let's say that it was.

Potatoes anchor a menu, grounding it in the certainty that this is dinner, freeing up the rest of the dishes to be as frivolous as they like, secure in the knowledge that nobody will be going home hungry. Other things do this too, of course – risotto, pasta, bread or polenta – but the potato has a special place in the Irish food psyche. The dishes here are some that have been staples on Paradiso menus over the years, mostly as side dishes, sometimes as tapas-y small plates and occasionally as a course in their own right.

potato pavé, caper dillisk aioli

serves 6–8

800g floury potatoes (see the tip)
50ml olive oil

TO FINISH:
caper dillisk aioli (page 185)

Preheat the oven to 180°C fan.

Scrub the potatoes well and trim off any blemishes or tough skin, then slice the potatoes thinly on a mandoline. In a bowl, mix together the sliced potatoes, the olive oil and a generous seasoning of salt and black pepper.

Layer the potatoes into a standard non-stick loaf tin (22cm × 12cm) and cook in the oven for approx. 1 hour. Check after 50 minutes by pushing a knife into the centre – you should feel no resistance if the pavé is cooked through.

Remove the pavé from the oven, place a second tin on top and put a heavy weight in the top tin. Leave overnight in the fridge.

After pressing overnight, turn the pavé out onto a chopping board and cut into six or eight slices.

Heat the oil in a deep-fryer to 170°C. Drop in the pavé slices a couple at a time and fry for 5–6 minutes, until crisp and golden.

Serve with caper dillisk aioli on the side and a pinch of flaky sea salt on top.

The recipe fills a standard non-stick loaf tin (22cm × 12cm) but you will need a second tin to press the pavé overnight.

This is best made from a potato that is maybe 7 or 8 on the flouriness scale, one that has enough starch for the thin slices to stick together but not so much that they become one mess of mash. We mostly use Roosters. Leave the skin on if it's thin and clean.

purple potatoes, chimichurri, soured cream

serves 4

500g purple potatoes
4 tablespoons soured cream
chimichurri (page 195)

Preheat the oven to 180°C fan.

Halve the purple potatoes and toss with olive oil and salt in an oven tray. Roast in the oven for 20–30 minutes, until tender.

To serve, spread some soured cream on each plate. Arrange the roast potato halves on top and drizzle over some chimichurri.

crushed potato, black sesame mayo

serves 4

1kg floury potatoes, peeled

TO FINISH:
2 spring onions, thinly sliced
black sesame mayo (page 185)

Chop the potatoes into quarters and steam them until soft. Leave to cool a little, then break them up with your hands.

Heat a generous amount of olive oil in a heavy-based frying pan over a high heat. Add the potatoes and fry them until browned, all the time turning them and coarsely mashing them with the side of a fish slice. The result should be a chunky mash with crisped shards throughout. Season well with salt and pepper.

To serve, spoon the crushed potato onto plates, sprinkle the sliced spring onions over and drizzle some black sesame mayo on the plate.

This is best made with a potato that is maybe 7 or 8 on the flouriness scale.

horseradish mash

serves 4

1kg floury potatoes, peeled
80g butter
150ml milk
1 × 4–6cm piece of fresh horseradish root (see the tip)

Chop the potatoes into roughly equal-sized chunks. Steam until soft, then pass the potatoes through a potato ricer or mash them.

Warm the butter and milk in a large pot, then add the potatoes and fold in. Finely grate the horseradish into the mash and season well with salt.

Use a very floury potato, such as Kerr's Pink, Maris Piper, Queens or Roosters.

You will need 1–1.5cm of horseradish root per person.

Mash is best made just before serving. However, if making it a little ahead, add the horseradish after reheating as it can lose its potency quickly.

pink fir apples, herbs, smoked tomato crumb

serves 4

500g Pink Fir Apple potatoes

TO FINISH:
green herb sauce (page 183)
smoked tomato crumb (page 171)

GARNISH:
fresh basil, dill, chives and fennel fronds

Preheat the oven to 180°C fan.

Wash the potatoes and slice them in half lengthways (or in three thick slices if very large). Trim a little slice off the skin edges to give them a small flat base.

Toss the potatoes in a little olive oil and salt and spread them on a parchment-lined oven tray. Roast in the oven for 20–30 minutes, until crisped and cooked through.

Fry some fresh basil leaves in olive oil for 20–30 seconds, until crisp. Drain on kitchen paper.

Arrange the roast potatoes on plates and add some blobs of green herb sauce. Sprinkle over little mounds of smoked tomato crumb and garnish with the fried basil leaves and fresh herbs.

paradiso fries

I wasn't going to include this as these old favourites haven't been on the menu for a while at the time of writing. Also, the method is a bit weird and is something that just evolved over the decades. I don't think this is how anyone else makes chips – hence the name, which is more confessional than proprietorial. But it makes great chips, ones that have been much loved down the years. It's difficult to replicate at home as you really need two fryers on the go at the same time, one at a lower temperature and one to finish the chips at a higher one. But you asked for it – at least some of you did, anyway.

2kg large Maris Piper potatoes, peeled

TO SERVE:
aioli or mayo

Preheat the oven to 150°C fan.

Trim the sides and ends of the potatoes to get a rectangular block. Save the trimmings to add to soup. Cut the blocks into smaller blocks 2cm on all sides and 7–10cm long. Put these in a bowl and toss them in a little vegetable oil – just enough to coat them – and some salt.

Line one or two oven trays with a generous overlap of parchment and place the oiled blocks on the tray(s) in a single layer. They can be close together but not piled up. Fold the overlapping parchment over to loosely close the package and put the tray(s) in the oven for 1 hour, until the potatoes are almost fully cooked through but uncoloured. Remove from the oven and leave to cool.

Heat the oil in a deep-fryer to 170°C. Add some of the partially cooked chips and fry for 8–10 minutes, until lightly coloured and fully cooked inside. Lift them out of the fryer and leave to rest again for 10 minutes.

Turn the fryer up to 190°C. Put the chips back in and cook for 5–7 minutes more, until well browned and crisp. Transfer to a tray lined with kitchen paper and season generously with flaky sea salt.

Serve with aioli or mayo and more flaky sea salt.

THERE IS A SIMPLE RULE to the structure of our dessert menu: chocolate, lemon, seasonal fruit. If there are more than three sweet offerings, then it's probably because there are two seasonal fruits demanding attention at the same time. That, or someone in the kitchen wants to try making dessert from a vegetable. Pumpkins, carrots and beetroot have been known to cross the line for brief dalliances in the desserts section, and there was once talk of turnips – well, they do have quite a sweet element, so perhaps we'll get back to that. But mostly we stick to the mantra of chocolate, lemon, seasonal fruit, and the passage of a year is marked by the procession of blood oranges, rhubarb, gooseberry, strawberry, blackberry, apple, damson and pear. Occasional notable guests include figs, quince, blackcurrants and plums. The recipes here are a small representation of one such year.

sweet

blood orange posset

serves 6

POSSET:
240ml blood orange juice
750ml cream
100g caster sugar
zest of 2 blood oranges
¼ teaspoon citric acid

DRIED BLOOD ORANGES:
1–2 blood oranges
a little caster sugar

MERINGUE SHEETS:
60ml egg whites (2–3 eggs)
90g caster sugar
30g glucose syrup
60ml water
½ teaspoon beetroot powder (page 174)

TO FINISH:
burnt orange sauce (page 189)

To make the posset, reduce the blood orange juice by half to 120ml in a small pan over a low heat. In a separate pan, boil the cream, sugar and zest for 1 minute, then add the reduced orange juice and the citric acid. Bring to a boil again, then remove the pan from the heat. Strain, discarding the zest, and leave the liquid for 10 minutes to partially cool. Pour into six small bowls or glasses and leave to set overnight or for at least 4 hours in the fridge.

To prepare the dried blood oranges, cut one or two blood oranges into thin slices (approx. 2mm). Place them on a dehydrator tray, sprinkle lightly with sugar and dehydrate overnight or until crisp.

To make the meringue sheets, whip the egg whites to stiff peaks. Heat the sugar, glucose and water to 118°C in a small pot. With the egg whisk running at high speed, slowly add the hot sugar mix. Continue whipping at a lower speed until the mix has cooled – test by touching the outside of the mixing bowl. Spread a thin layer of meringue on a dehydrator sheet and sprinkle the beetroot powder over it. Dehydrate for 4 hours in the dehydrator. Break or cut the crisp meringue into shards.

To serve, place a tablespoon of burnt orange sauce on top of each set posset and arrange the dried orange and meringue shards on top.

poached rhubarb, brûlée crème fraîche tart

makes 12–20 slices

PASTRY:

250g cold unsalted butter, diced
250g plain flour

50g icing sugar
1 egg, beaten

TART FILLING:

6 eggs
300g caster sugar
25g plain flour
300ml cream

1kg crème fraîche, strained
  overnight for best results
zest of 2 oranges
icing sugar, to finish

POACHED RHUBARB:

150g caster sugar
500ml water
150ml white wine
4 hibiscus flowers

2 pieces of candied stem ginger
juice of ½ lemon
4–6 sticks of rhubarb

Make the pastry by cutting the butter into the flour to get a fine crumb, then folding in the icing sugar and beaten egg. Knead quickly to get a smooth dough. Refrigerate for 1 hour, then roll out and press into an oiled 32cm round, fluted, loose-based tin. Refrigerate again for at least 1 hour.

Preheat the oven to 160°C fan. Line the pastry with a piece of non-stick baking paper and fill it with baking beans.

Blind bake the pastry in the preheated oven until just lightly coloured, then remove from the oven and cool on a wire rack.

To make the tart filling, beat the eggs and caster sugar together with a pinch of salt. Stir in the flour, then the cream, the crème fraîche and finally the orange zest. Fill the pastry case with the crème fraîche mix. Bake the tart in the oven for 1 hour or so, until the filling is set. Remove and leave to cool.

To poach the rhubarb, put everything except the rhubarb in a pot and bring to a boil. Remove from the heat and leave to steep for 1 hour.

Preheat the oven to 150°C fan. Trim the ends of the rhubarb and slice into 10cm lengths. Line an oven tray with parchment, allowing enough overhang to fully cover the contents. Place the rhubarb slices in the tray. Bring the poaching liquid back to a boil and pour it over the rhubarb. Fold over the parchment to make a loosely sealed parcel. Place this in the oven to poach the rhubarb. Check after 10 minutes and again every 5 minutes afterwards. When the rhubarb is just tender, remove the tray from the oven and leave to cool. Remove the rhubarb from the liquid. Place some of the liquid back on the hob and reduce to a syrup.

To serve, sprinkle the top of the tart with icing sugar and use a kitchen blowtorch to caramelise it. Place a slice of tart on a plate with a piece of rhubarb beside it and pour a little of the rhubarb syrup over.

strawberry & elderflower pavlova

serves 6

PAVLOVAS:
120g egg whites
220g caster sugar, divided

1 teaspoon cornflour
1 teaspoon white wine vinegar

STRAWBERRY CONSOMMÉ:
300g strawberries, chopped
60g caster sugar

ELDERFLOWER CREAM:
200ml cream
20g caster sugar

1 teaspoon elderflower cordial

TO FINISH:
18–20 strawberries, halved or
   quartered

basil oil (page 196)
edible flowers

To make the pavlovas, preheat the oven to 130°C fan.

Whip the egg whites to soft peaks, then slowly add 170g of the sugar, beating in 1 tablespoon or so every 30 seconds at first, then 2 tablespoons at a time until all 170g has been used.

Mix together the remaining 50g sugar and the cornflour. Add this to the whipping meringue, 2 tablespoons at a time. Scrape down the sides of the bowl, add the vinegar and continue whipping for 5 minutes. Put the meringue in a piping bag.

Line an oven tray with parchment. Lightly oil a 7cm metal ring and place it on the parchment. Pipe some meringue into the ring, filling it and swirling the top to get a flat-ish top. Lift off the ring, wipe it clean, oil it again and repeat to make six pavlovas in total.

Place the tray in the oven and bake for 12 minutes, then lower the heat to 80°C fan and bake for 12 minutes more. Turn off the heat and leave for another 12 minutes. Finally, open the oven door and leave for 12 minutes. Remove the pavlovas from the oven and leave to cool completely. Use a palette knife to carefully remove the pavlovas from the tray.

To make the strawberry consommé, put the strawberries and sugar in a metal bowl and seal the top. Place over a pot of boiling water for 40 minutes to soften the fruit. Transfer the fruit mix to a sieve lined with cheesecloth and strain over a bowl for 2 hours, retaining the liquid.

To make the elderflower cream, whip the cream with the sugar, adding the elderflower cordial at the end.

To serve, place a pavlova on each plate with the flatter side up. Top with elderflower cream and halved or quartered strawberries, then pour a thin pool of strawberry consommé around the pavlova. Add a small amount of basil oil around the edge of the consommé, then scatter over a few mint leaves and edible flowers.

chocolate, blackberry, honeycomb, pistachio

serves 8

CHOCOLATE MOUSSE:
150ml aquafaba
40g caster sugar
¼ teaspoon xanthan gum

150g dark chocolate, chopped
½ teaspoon vanilla extract
125g almond milk

BLACKBERRIES:
200g blackberries
50g caster sugar

1 teaspoon lemon juice

CHOCOLATE SHARDS:
15g freeze-dried blackberries
50g dark chocolate

TO FINISH:
honeycomb crisp (page 174)
1 tablespoon chopped toasted pistachios

To make the chocolate mousse, whisk the aquafaba, sugar and xanthan gum to soft peaks. Put the chocolate and vanilla in a heatproof bowl with a pinch of salt. Bring the almond milk to a boil, then pour it over the chocolate. Cover and leave for 5 minutes, then stir the chocolate and milk together until smooth and the chocolate has melted. Leave for 2–3 minutes for the mix to cool slightly, then fold in the aquafaba mixture 1 tablespoon at a time. Grease 8 × 6cm round or square metal rings with oil and set them on a parchment-lined tray. Pour the mousse into the greased rings and place in the fridge to set for approx. 4 hours.

To prepare the blackberries, set aside half of the fruit. Put the other half in a pot with the sugar and lemon juice and bring to a boil. Reduce the heat to low and simmer for 10 minutes. Blend the sauce, pass it through a fine sieve and leave to cool.

To make the chocolate shards, chop the freeze-dried blackberries finely by pulsing in a food processor. Melt the dark chocolate in a heatproof bowl set over a pan of gently simmering water, then stir in the blackberries. Place a large sheet of parchment paper on a cool flat surface and pour on the chocolate. Add another sheet of parchment on top and roll the chocolate evenly between the sheets until it's about 2mm thin. Place it on a tray and allow to cool. You can speed this up by putting the tray in a fridge or freezer. When cool, crack the chocolate into irregular shards.

To serve, warm the sides of the rings with a blowtorch, then lift off the rings and carefully transfer the mousse to plates. Decorate with the fresh blackberries, blackberry sauce, chocolate shards, pieces of honeycomb crisp and chopped pistachios.

damson mascarpone ice cream, dried pear, ricky o'reilly

serves 8

Ricky O'Reillys are a soft almond biscuit closely related to their Italian cousins, the ricciarelli clan.

DAMSON MASCARPONE ICE CREAM:

500g whole damsons
100g light muscovado sugar
50g caster sugar
100ml water
pinch of nutmeg

pinch of ground cinnamon
160g icing sugar
4 egg yolks
500g mascarpone
1 teaspoon vanilla extract

DRIED PEAR:

2 pears
juice of ½ lemon

RICKY O'REILLYS:

2 egg whites
300g ground almonds
250g caster sugar

100g icing sugar, plus a little
  more to finish
zest of 1 orange
1 teaspoon baking powder

To make the ice cream, put the damsons, sugars and water in a pot and bring to a boil, then lower the heat to a simmer and cook gently for 8–10 minutes, until the fruit is soft. Pass through a coarse sieve to remove the damson stones, then add the spices and blend to a fine purée. Leave to cool.

Whisk the icing sugar and egg yolks until light and fluffy, then gently fold in the mascarpone and vanilla. Churn in an ice cream machine until softly frozen. Line a freezer-safe container and layer in the ice cream and damson sauce, starting and finishing with the ice cream. Freeze.

To make the dried pear, cut the pear lengthways into slices 2mm thick. Brush the slices with lemon juice and place them in a dehydrator at 60°C for 2–3 hours, until crisp. Leave to cool.

To make the Ricky O'Reillys, whisk the egg whites to soft peaks. Add the ground almonds, sugars, orange zest and baking powder and mix with a wooden spoon. Use a wet spoon to shape the mixture into small ovals. Place these on a parchment-lined oven tray and leave to dry out for 2 hours.

Preheat the oven to 160°C fan. Bake the biscuits for 30–35 minutes, until risen and lightly golden. Remove from the oven and sift icing sugar over them while they're still hot, then leave to cool.

To serve, decorate one or two scoops of the ice cream with a slice of dried pear and add one or two biscuits alongside.

roast figs, lemon cardamom polenta cake, sweet almond cream

serves 4–6

LEMON CARDAMOM POLENTA CAKE:
115g ground almonds
115g fine polenta
1 tablespoon baking powder
½ teaspoon baking soda
10 cardamom pods, seeds only, finely ground
¼ teaspoon xanthan gum
110ml sunflower oil
150g caster sugar
zest of 2 lemons
190g coconut yogurt

LEMON SYRUP:
juice of 2 lemons
50g icing sugar

ROAST FIGS:
8 black figs, halved
2 tablespoons olive oil
1 tablespoon pomegranate molasses

TO FINISH:
sweet almond cream (page 203)

To make the polenta cake, preheat the oven to 150°C fan.

Combine the ground almonds, polenta, baking powder, baking soda, ground cardamom, xanthan gum and a pinch of salt in a bowl.

Separately, whisk together the oil, sugar and lemon zest, then stir in the yogurt.

Fold the wet ingredients into the dry and pour the mix into an oiled 21cm × 15cm tray. Bake in the oven for 30 minutes, until just set. Remove the cake from the oven and prick it all over with a toothpick or cake tester.

Warm the lemon juice and icing sugar together until the sugar has just melted, then slowly pour this syrup over the cake to get an even distribution. Leave to cool.

To roast the figs, toss the halved figs in the olive oil. Heat a griddle pan or heavy-based frying pan over a high heat and place the figs on it, cut side down. Cook for 3–4 minutes, until the figs are coloured or lined on the cut side. Turn them over and cook for 2 minutes more. Transfer the grilled figs to a bowl and toss them with the pomegranate molasses.

Whip the almond cream with a whisk, adding a little almond milk if required to get a soft whipped consistency.

To serve, nestle the figs on top of some almond cream with a drizzle of the pomegranate juices and place a piece of polenta cake alongside.

04

MOSTLY, BY STAFF WE MEAN the kitchen crew. The front of house will usually be served dishes from the menu or variations on them. The kitchen rarely eats like that. After a busy night of plating up the menu dishes over and over again, of repeatedly tasting the sauces and checking the textures, tired minds and bodies want something else. Something not knife-and-fork food. Something comforting cobbled together from a raid across the sections or an unlikely concoction that delivers enough flavour impact to reach and satisfy over-exercised taste buds. Horseradish mash with lime curry, anyone?

For the daytime prep chefs, it's about time. Sometimes their day has in-built time to make a favourite dish to feed themselves and anyone else who happens to be around; other days that time is stolen by the workload and lunch is improvised in five minutes from scraps of the morning's prep. In the evening too, sometimes all a chef can pull together is a sandwich, eaten sitting on the flour bin. Still a decent sandwich, though.

That's the thing. There's always loads of stuff to make a meal from. Staff meals in a restaurant are like the ultimate back-of-the-fridge cooking, where the fridge in question has an almost bottomless variety of sauces, carbs, proteins, vegetables, pickles and preserves, not to mention complex crunchy toppings too. Sometimes it's every man, woman and child for themselves but usually someone knocks something together that will satisfy the team. As much as chefs like to impress customers in the dining room, there's nothing like a thumbs up from another chef who can't stop eating to speak.

The recipes in this chapter cover all these variations on the staff dinner and, with a couple of exceptions, they are mostly just one take on endless improvisations. The things they all have in common are that they taste great and they easily multiply up or down, depending on how many mouths there are to feed.

staff dinner

dan dan noodles

serves 4–6

This highly spiced dish is a little bit of work if you're making it from scratch but if most of the elements are to hand, it can be put together in 15 minutes. The separately cooked elements of tofu mix, sauce, noodles and greens are layered into bowls for the eater to mix themselves. This results in the rare pleasure of a dish that keeps getting better and more intensely flavoured as you eat into it, and the last mouthful is often the best. There aren't many dishes you can say that about!

We use tahini as the base simply because there is always some around and we've come to like the light, creamy finish it gives. Chinese sesame paste, if you can find or make it, will give a darker, more robust appearance and flavour.

½ aubergine, finely diced
4 mushrooms, diced
100g napa cabbage stalk, finely
    chopped
2 garlic cloves, sliced
250g tofu, crumbled

1 tablespoon hoisin sauce
1 tablespoon Shaoxing cooking
    wine
1 teaspoon soy sauce
½ teaspoon Chinese five-spice

SAUCE:
100g tahini
150ml water
40ml soy sauce

½ teaspoon Chinese five-spice
150ml dan dan oil (page 195)

TO FINISH:
400g rice or wheat noodles
steamed pak choi or other greens

To make the sauce, whisk together the tahini, water, soy sauce and five-spice in a small pot over a low heat until emulsified, then slowly whisk in the dan dan oil, adding more water if required. Set aside.

Fry the aubergine in oil until browned and almost fully cooked. Add the mushrooms, cabbage stalk and garlic and cook for a few minutes more. Add the tofu and continue to cook until everything is nicely browned. Stir in the hoisin, Shaoxing cooking wine, soy sauce and five-spice and cook for 1 minute, then remove the pan from the heat.

Cook the noodles according to the packet instructions.

To serve, place a spoonful of the tofu mix in a bowl. Add some warmed sauce, then the noodles, then some steamed greens and finally a little more sauce.

zhoug maltagliati

serves 4

Maltagliati means roughly cut, and in the Paradiso kitchen this simple dish is made from the offcuts and scraps of fresh pasta after making tortellini or cappelloni. Zhoug may seem like an unlikely pasta sauce until you think of it as a coriander pesto with a kick of chilli and a hint of the exotic in cardamom that drags the pasta out of its comfort zone and off down the coast to meet new friends.

Walnut crumb – it's worth repeating – tastes good on everything. If you keep a jar in the fridge, you'll be able to give any dish a complex finish in no time at all.

400g fresh pasta
4 handfuls of chopped cavolo nero or other greens
4 tablespoons zhoug (page 195)
80g Knockalara fresh sheep's cheese or feta
4 tablespoons walnut crumb (page 170)

Cook the fresh pasta. At the same time, sauté the greens in olive oil. Add the cooked pasta to the cooked greens in the pot and stir in the zhoug. Season with salt.

Serve in bowls topped with some crumbled cheese and a sprinkling of walnut crumb.

beluga bowl

serves 4

This most frequent staff dinner is based on the presumption that there are some braised beluga lentils hanging around. Making it at home from scratch, simply boil some lentils and start from the second cooking stage, where they are briefly finished in a rich stock. Here it is fennel and smoky tomato. Other variations depend on what happens to be near to hand and include ginger broth, hazelnut rayu and cashew korma.

While the lentils are warming through in their secondary stock, we prepare the other toppings. These typically include something of substance, such as potatoes, polenta or squash; a rich protein like halloumi, mozzarella or egg; a roasted vegetable, perhaps carrot, beetroot, aubergine or the fennel here; and sometimes a fresh green. The dish is finished with something to add zing or spice, such as zhoug, chermoula or pickles, and a crunch, such as one of the crumbs or a sprinkle of nuts.

This lentil bowl is descended from cuchara de comida, the Spanish concept of spoon food, introduced to the kitchen during the reign of Eneko Lopez as head chef. All the ingredients should be chopped so that the dish can be eaten with a spoon, or at least one-handed without the need of a knife. But no matter how much stuff you throw at it, the finished dish should remain primarily a bowl of highly flavoured lentils.

2 heads of fennel, braised as per
   page 112
50g smoked tomato purée
   (page 187)
a little stock or water
400g braised beluga lentils
   (page 199)
4 purple potatoes, peeled,
   chopped and steamed

4 slices of halloumi
a squeeze of fresh lime juice
2 tablespoons chermoula
   (page 194)
2 tablespoons smoked tomato
   crumb (page 171)
a handful of fresh coriander
   leaves

Blend half of one of the braised fennel bulbs with the smoked tomato purée and a little stock or water. Put this enriched stock in a wide pot with the braised beluga lentils and warm them over a low heat.

Slice the remaining braised fennel lengthways into two or three wedges, depending on their thickness. Place these on an oven tray with the steamed purple potatoes and place in an oven to warm through.

Fry the halloumi slices in a little olive oil, finishing them with a dash of lime juice in the pan, then chop them into small chunks.

To serve, place the warm lentils in shallow bowls and top each portion with some fennel, potato and halloumi. Dot with a little more smoked tomato purée, drizzle over some chermoula and sprinkle over some smoked tomato crumb and fresh coriander.

rice paper salad rolls, almond satay dip

makes 8

Summer sandwiches crammed with green things, herbs, tofu and the zing of sushi ginger.

8 rice paper rolls

FILLING:
4 handfuls of shredded cabbage and/or thinly sliced pak choi
a handful of grated carrots
½ cucumber, thinly sliced
a handful of cooked and chopped vermicelli noodles
6 slices of chilli-glazed tofu (page 84), thinly sliced
6 pieces of sushi ginger, thinly sliced
2 handfuls of a mix of fresh coriander, mint and basil

SATAY DIP:
juice of 1 lime
4 tablespoons almond satay (page 68)

Mix all the filling ingredients together.

Dip each rice paper roll into a shallow bowl of warm water for 20–30 seconds to soften it. Lay it flat on a towel, then transfer to a work surface.

Place a small handful of the filling near the end that's closest to you and roll up to almost halfway, keeping the filling tight as you go. Fold in the sides and roll to the end to make a sealed parcel. Repeat to make eight rolls. Cut each roll in half on the diagonal.

To make the satay dip, add the lime juice to the almond satay and whisk in some water to get a thin dipping sauce.

Serve three or four half-rolls per person with individual dipping bowls of the satay dip.

Ro's tortilla

serves 8–10

Ro's been making tortilla since she was able to reach the stove by standing on her rocking horse. A recipe for tortilla is a simple thing but making it well requires a bit of practice and an understanding of what you're trying to achieve. That's true of a lot of food, possibly more so the simpler a dish appears to be.

While there is a fashion for runny tortilla made in small pans for one or two people, this large, firmer one is made to be laid out for people to serve themselves over the following hour or so, as they come to gaps in their prep work or arrive for the start of a shift. A firmer tortilla is also great for picnics and parties.

1.5kg medium floury potatoes
 (such as Roosters), weighed
 after peeling

1 large onion
12 eggs

TO SERVE:
date jam (page 189)
aioli or mayo

sautéed kale or spinach

Cut the peeled potatoes in half and slice them thinly, approx. 3mm thick. Halve and slice the onion the same way.

In a heavy-based frying pan (see the tip), heat enough oil to cover the potatoes. Add the sliced potatoes and onion and cook over a medium heat, stirring often, until the potatoes are tender but not coloured.

Meanwhile, whisk the eggs in a large bowl. Drain the potatoes and onion, saving the oil (see the tip), and stir them into the eggs. Season well with salt.

Heat the pan again over a low heat and brush it very lightly with olive oil. Pour in the potato and egg mix and leave to cook slowly for 8–10 minutes. Lift the edge carefully with a spatula now and then to check its progress. When the underside is beginning to colour and the egg seems fairly well set, cover the pan with a large plate or tray and quickly turn it over so that the tortilla is on the plate, then slide the tortilla back into the pan. Tuck the edges down and return the pan to the heat to cook slowly for 8–10 minutes more.

When you are satisfied that the tortilla is just set, slide it onto a plate and leave to cool for a few minutes.

Cut into wedges and serve warm or at room temperature. Serve with date jam, a simple aioli or mayo, and a pile of sautéed kale or spinach.

We make this in a large 30cm wide pan that makes enough for 8–10 people. For a standard domestic 24cm pan, you would need a little over half the recipe.

The oil for frying the potatoes can be reused a number of times. The process is more boiling in oil than deep-frying.

John's soup

serves 4

This is a comforting soup/stew cross that gets its depth from a braise of vegetables at the start, a good stock and from being half blended at the end.

Once the basic soup is made, it can then become as exciting as you like with the addition of any condiments and toppings that you have to hand. We would usually put some or all of these on the table for everyone to build their own finished dish: pepper harissa, smoky za'atar, chermoula, jalapeño butter, grated hard cheese, crumbled soft cheese, walnut crumb, lemony borlotti or chickpeas, romesco. I suppose this is a good time and place to reveal the truism that there is no soup that is not improved by a spoon of yogurt and a swirl of dan dan oil.

5 medium shallots, halved and thinly sliced
4 medium carrots, peeled, quartered lengthways and diced
1 large ripe tomato, roughly chopped
6 garlic cloves, thinly sliced
4 sprigs of fresh thyme
100ml white wine
1.3 litres vegetable stock
350g potato, peeled and diced into 1cm cubes
a small handful of offcuts of other veg, such as cauliflower, squash
    or turnip
a large handful of chopped greens, such as kale, cabbage, broccoli
    or chard
a small handful of fresh herbs, such as basil, marjoram or oregano
50g salted butter

TO SERVE:
focaccia

Heat some oil in a pot. Add the shallots, carrots, tomato, garlic and thyme and sweat together for 10 minutes over a low heat. Add the white wine and simmer for 5 minutes to reduce. Add the vegetable stock and bring to a boil, then reduce the heat back down to low and simmer for 40 minutes.

At the same time, steam the diced potato and any offcuts of other veg that require longer cooking. Add these to the pot along with the greens, herbs and any remaining tender offcuts. Simmer for a few minutes more to soften the greens. Remove the thyme stems.

Remove one large ladleful of soup to a jug, add the butter and use a stick blender to blend to a purée. Return this to the pot and season well with salt and black pepper.

Bowl up, as John would say, and enjoy. Serve with thickly cut salty focaccia.

summer lasagne, sungold salsa

serves 6–8

Use a combination of melting and hard cheeses. We use Templegall or Coolea with Cáis na Tíre or Cratloe Hills.

500g peeled potatoes, thinly sliced
750g courgettes, thinly sliced
2 shallots, thinly sliced
8 garlic cloves, thinly sliced

50g fresh basil, sliced
1 tablespoon fresh thyme leaves
100ml tomato passata
600g fresh pasta sheets

CHEESE SAUCE:
70g butter
70g plain flour
1 dessertspoon Dijon mustard

800ml milk
350g grated cheese (see the intro)

TO FINISH:
sungold salsa (page 188)

Bring a pot of salted water to a boil. Add the potatoes, bring back to a boil and simmer for 2–3 minutes. Transfer the almost-cooked potato slices to a bowl of cold water.

Mix the courgettes, shallots, garlic and herbs together. Heat some olive oil in a wide pan over a high heat. Fry the courgette mix in batches until lightly cooked. Season with salt and black pepper.

To make the sauce, melt the butter in a pan, add the flour and cook for a few minutes over a low heat, stirring. Add the mustard and cook for a few seconds more. Whisk in some of the milk and bring it to a boil, then add some more milk and repeat until all the milk has been used and you have a thickened sauce with a rich pouring consistency. Add the grated cheese – holding back 50g for finishing the dish – and stir until melted. Season well with salt and black pepper.

Preheat the oven to 180°C fan.

To assemble, combine the passata with 1 tablespoon of olive oil and spread it on the bottom of a 30 × 24cm lasagne dish. Build the lasagne like so: pasta sheets, courgettes, a drizzle of cheese sauce; pasta sheets, potato, cheese sauce; pasta sheets, courgette, cheese sauce; pasta sheets, potato, cheese sauce; pasta sheets, courgette; pasta sheets. Finish with a generous blanket of cheese sauce and a sprinkling of the reserved cheese.

Cook in the oven for 30 minutes. Check, then cook for a further 15–20 minutes, reducing the heat to 160°C fan if the top is browning too quickly. Remove from the oven and leave to rest for 15–20 minutes before slicing.

To serve, spoon some salsa, including the liquid, over each portion of lasagne.

tofu, aubergine & napa cabbage curry

serves 4

This is essentially a quick curry made by adding readily at-hand ingredients to the coconut tamarind broth we serve with the chilli-glazed tofu on page 84. The sauce is thinnish and creamy and is best served over noodles, though it also works with rice or bread, especially if you cook it down to be a little thicker.

1 large aubergine
450g tofu
2 tablespoons soy sauce
½ head of napa cabbage, sliced
coconut tamarind broth (page 191)
250g tinned chickpeas (net weight of 1 × 400g tin)
a handful of chopped fresh coriander

TO SERVE:
hot sauce
pickled red onion (page 178) or pickled radish (page 180)

Preheat the oven to 200°C fan.

Chop the aubergine into 3cm chunks. Toss in olive oil in an oven dish and roast in the oven for 15–20 minutes, stirring once or twice, until well done.

At the same time, tear the tofu into small irregular pieces. Heat some oil in a large frying pan or wok and fry the tofu, stirring often, until crisp and browned. Stir in the soy sauce, then transfer the tofu to a bowl.

In the same pan, fry the sliced cabbage for 3–4 minutes, until just tender.

Heat the coconut tamarind broth in a pot and add the aubergine, tofu, cabbage and chickpeas. Bring to a boil and add the chopped coriander.

Serve with a hot sauce on the table for those who like more kick to their curry and a bowl of pickles, such as red onion or radish.

turnip sandwiches

This is a posh version of an old Cork country dish made with boiled turnip slices and flavoured with white pepper and brown sauce. We make these using the turnip slices from the braised turnip galette on page 90, where the turnip has been cooked slowly in white wine, butter and maple syrup. If you're making that dish, braise a few extra slices of turnip for tomorrow's breakfast or lunch.

Of course everyone makes their own variation, but the thing is to remember that it's all about the turnip. As a wise old woman was tired of pointing out, there's no point in putting turnip in a sandwich if you can't taste the turnip. That said, popular additions include pickled fennel, fried mushrooms, fresh sheep's cheese, date jam, smoked tomato, walnuts, cold miso gravy and even kimchi, but that last one only by the kind of people who put kimchi in everything.

This version is reasonably faithful to the traditional one of turnip, bread, butter and a savoury sauce. I hardly need to tell you how to make a sandwich, but this is how we make ours. For each sandwich, we use two slices of braised turnip (page 90), warmed through in an oven or frying pan, and some beetroot harissa (page 187) on well-buttered crusty white bread.

05

THERE ARE TWO PARTS to the day of a restaurant kitchen. There's the one you see sometimes, especially now that so many kitchens are open and the diners are almost an audience to the players making dinner: chefs crouched over a line of plates, hurriedly yet patiently making each one as close to perfect as the speeding time allows, juggling pots and pans at the same time. From the moment the first order arrives, it is all one big connected dance, with dozens of tiny internal timers constantly going off. Move this, flip that, put the crunchy stuff on those, start that while finishing this. Pulling it off over a sustained number of hours, day after day, requires a peculiar combination of skills and a fierce sense of organisation. It only works if everything is where it's supposed to be every single time. And the prep has to be good. Above all, the prep must be good.

Early every morning, while the service chefs are having a lie-in or doing their yoga, the other part of a restaurant's day begins. The prep chefs arrive, crank up the kitchen and check their lists. Their day is governed not by the thousand little internal timers, but by the big clock that says you've got this number of hours to have that lot perfectly cooked, packed up, portioned, labelled. This is when the building blocks of the dishes are made. The pumpkin seed mole that the evening chefs only need to spread on plates, the al dente beluga lentils with just the right touch of thyme and red wine, the crunchy stuff, pickles and dressings, the perfectly blanched vegetables and partially cooked seven-minutes-to-finish risotto.

The recipes in this chapter are how this prep work is done. Before you can make the plates in the first part of the book, you will need to make some of the core elements here. Most can be made in advance, often days ahead. Make a list, form a plan and work through the elements, then before you know it a dish is more than halfway done.

Some of these elements are used on a variety of dishes, while others are designed for just one specific dish. Don't let that stop you finding your own uses for them.

crunchy stuff

It started with the spiced walnut crumb, originally created to deliver a kick of spice and, yes, crunch to a comfortingly soft risotto. In time, crunch became part of the language of building a dish, meaning something that adds texture as the final element. But crunchy stuff also delivers a flavour hit within that texture. Sat around the long table at the back of the dining room, with notebook pages filling up with scratched sketches and crossed-out words, elements being added and taken back out until we're nearly there, someone will inevitably suggest the walnut crumb to cap it off. It's already on the menu on something else, of course. 'We need a new crunchy thing, then...'

Most of the crunchy stuff is multi-purpose and lasts a long time. The best approach is to make a batch of one, store it in a dry, tightly sealed container and discover for yourself what you like to put it on.

walnut crumb

makes 2 small jars

2 tablespoons coriander seeds
2 teaspoons fennel seeds
5 dried bird's eye chillies
250g day-old white bread
200g walnuts
2 tablespoons fresh thyme leaves

Grind the seeds and chillies.

Put the bread, walnuts and thyme in a food processor and chop to a uniform crumb texture. Add the ground spices and chillies and a little salt and pulse to mix.

Heat a little olive oil in a heavy-based frying pan over a medium heat. Working in batches, add the crumb mix and fry until crisp, stirring often. Finish by drying in a low oven if necessary. Leave to cool fully before storing in clean sealed jars.

Keeps for up to four weeks in a dry sealed jar.

hazelnut crumb

makes 1 small jar

50g skinned hazelnuts
50g breadcrumbs made from
   day-old bread
1 tablespoon fresh thyme leaves

Preheat the oven to 100°C fan.

Place the hazelnuts on a tray and toast in the oven for 15–20 minutes, until lightly browned. Chop the nuts coarsely by crushing them with the flat side of a wide knife or a rolling pin.

Place a frying pan on a medium heat. Add 1 tablespoon of olive oil and then the breadcrumbs. Toast until golden brown, stirring frequently. When the crumbs are crisp, add the nuts and thyme and toss everything together in the pan for a few seconds. Remove from the heat, season with salt and leave to cool.

Keeps for up to two weeks in a dry airtight container.

pine nut crumb

makes 1 small jar

50g pine nuts, coarsely chopped
50g breadcrumbs made from day-old
  bread
2 sprigs of fresh thyme, leaves stripped
  and finely chopped
10g finely grated hard sheep's cheese
  (optional)

Heat a heavy-based frying pan on a low
heat. Add the pine nuts, breadcrumbs
and thyme and toast them slowly,
stirring often, until golden and crisp.
Remove from the heat and leave to cool,
then season with salt and stir in the
cheese (if using).

Keeps for days in the fridge and
freezes well.

ras el hanout crumb

makes 1 small jar

50g panko breadcrumbs
1 teaspoon ras el hanout (page 201)

Heat a little olive oil in a heavy-based
frying pan over a medium heat. Add the
breadcrumbs and fry for 5–7 minutes,
until golden. Add the spice and a pinch
of salt and continue cooking for 1 minute
more. Remove from the heat and leave
to cool.

Keeps in a dry airtight container for a week
or more.

smoked tomato crumb

We get our smoked sun-dried tomatoes
from Olives West Cork.

makes 1 small jar

20g smoked sun-dried tomatoes
2 tablespoons extra virgin olive oil
100g breadcrumbs, made from day-old
  bread

Make a paste with the smoked tomatoes
using a food processor or a pestle and
mortar.
   Heat the oil in a heavy-based frying
pan over a medium heat. Add the
breadcrumbs and toast until golden
brown, tossing and stirring frequently.
When crisp, remove the crumbs to a
parchment-lined tray to cool.
   Preheat the oven to 60°C fan or turn
on a dehydrator.
   Transfer the crumbs to a bowl and stir
in the smoked tomato paste, using your
hands to fully combine the two. Season
with salt.
   Place this mixture back on the
parchment-lined tray and put it in the
oven or dehydrator to become dry and
crisp. This will take 1–2 hours. Allow to
cool completely.

Keeps for up to two weeks in a dry airtight
container.

pistachio dukkah

makes 1 small jar

2 teaspoons coriander seeds
1 teaspoon cumin seeds
½ teaspoon fennel seeds
20g pistachio nuts, roasted
15g hazelnuts, roasted
1 tablespoon fresh thyme leaves
1 tablespoon sesame seeds, lightly
    toasted
½ teaspoon black peppercorns,
    finely ground

Toast the coriander, cumin and fennel seeds together. Allow to cool, then coarsely grind them.

Finely chop the pistachios, hazelnuts and fresh thyme in a food processor. Add the sesame seeds, peppercorns and ground seeds and pulse briefly to combine.

Keeps for weeks in a dry airtight container.

salted walnuts

The salt in the title comes from the blanching as well as the seasoning.

fine sea salt and flaky sea salt
extra virgin olive oil
walnuts

Bring a pot of heavily salted water to a boil. Blanch some walnuts by putting them in a basket and lowering it into the water five times, each time for 10 seconds. Drain the walnuts and put them in a bowl with a little extra virgin olive oil and some flaky sea salt. Dry in a dehydrator or on a parchment-lined oven tray in a 50°C fan oven for 1 hour.

Keeps well for a week or more in a dry airtight container.

The walnuts can be used in halves or chopped smaller, depending on the use.

fried pumpkin seeds

Originally used to make pepitas crispbreads, we now use these as a base for the pumpkin seed mole on page 66. They are great as a snack or tossed over a salad – for those uses you can add other seasonings with the salt, such as Korean pepper flakes, ras el hanout or smoked paprika.

vegetable oil
pumpkin seeds
fine sea salt

Heat some vegetable oil in a large, wide, heavy-based pot. Drop in the pumpkin seeds to deep-fry until they start to pop. Remove the seeds to a tray lined with kitchen paper, then to a bowl. Season well with sea salt and leave to cool.

Keeps well for weeks in a dry airtight container.

fried peanuts

makes 150g

½ cinnamon stick
1 clove
1 star anise
1 teaspoon fennel seeds
1 teaspoon salt
1 teaspoon caster sugar
300ml sunflower oil
150g peanuts

Toast the cinnamon, clove, star anise and fennel seeds briefly. Leave to cool, then grind them together, adding the salt and sugar at the end.

Heat the sunflower oil to 180°C in a deep-fryer or pot and add the peanuts. Fry for 8–10 minutes, stirring often, until they turn golden brown. Remove the peanuts from the oil and toss with the spice mix. Allow to cool completely.

Keeps for up to a week in a dry airtight container.

crisped vermicelli

makes 8–10 portions

vegetable oil
20g thin vermicelli noodles

Heat some vegetable oil to 190°C in a large, wide, heavy-based pan. Drop a few noodles into the pan and swish them around with heatproof tongs. This gets them gathered together. When the noodles puff up after a few seconds, remove them from the oil and put them on a kitchen paper-lined tray to drain. Season with salt. Repeat with the rest of the noodles and allow to cool completely.

Keeps for a few days in a dry airtight container but are best made on the day.

popped barley

makes 10–15 portions

300ml vegetable oil
50g barley

Heat the oil to 190°C in a large, wide, heavy-based pan. Drop one piece of barley in the oil to test that the oil is hot enough to make the grain pop. When the oil is ready, drop in a quarter of the barley. When the grains have popped, remove them with a sieve, scatter them on a tray lined with kitchen paper and season with salt. Repeat with the rest of the barley in batches and allow the popped barley to cool fully.

Keeps for one week in a dry airtight container.

fried capers

makes 1 small jar

100g capers
vegetable oil

Drain the capers and pat them dry.
   Heat some vegetable oil in a deep-fryer or a large, wide, heavy-based pot to 170°C. Add the capers and fry until they stop sizzling, then remove them to a tray lined with kitchen paper to dry and cool fully.

Keeps for a few days in a dry airtight container.

crisped shallots

makes 8–12 portions as a garnish

2–3 large banana shallots, thinly sliced
   and separated

Heat some vegetable oil in a deep-fryer to 160°C. Working in batches, add a handful of shallot slices to the fryer and cook, stirring constantly, until they begin to turn golden. Remove the cooked slices, scatter on a tray lined with kitchen paper and sprinkle with a little salt. Repeat with the remaining shallot slices.
   The cooked slices will crisp as they cool but if they are not fully crisp when cooled, place them in an oven at 50°C fan for 1 hour to dry out.

Keeps for a week or two in a dry airtight container lined with kitchen paper.

dried olives

makes 1 small jar

150g Moroccan black olives, pitted

Chop the olives coarsely and place them on a parchment-lined baking sheet in a dehydrator or the oven at 60°C fan. They should be very dry after 8 hours.

Finely chop them in a food processor or with a sharp knife and return to the oven or dehydrator to dry to a crisp finish.

Keeps for up to a month in a dry airtight container in a cool, dark place.

beetroot powder

makes 1 small jar

This version starts with a whole beetroot. However, we usually make it from the pulp when we are juicing beets for braising beluga lentils or the beetroot port gravy on page 190. The powder is mostly used to add a swathe of colour to a plate, but if you want it to deliver some fire as well, add a little cayenne pepper.

1–2 beetroot

Peel and thinly slice one or two beetroot. Dehydrate in a dehydrator or overnight in an oven at a very low heat, approx. 50°C fan.

Blend to a fine powder in a food processor or spice grinder. If you want a fully uniform dust, pass through a fine sieve to discard any remaining slightly larger pieces.

Keeps very well in a dry airtight container.

honeycomb crisp

makes 8–10 portions

200g caster sugar
25g honey
½ teaspoon lemon juice
½ teaspoon water
2 teaspoons bicarbonate of soda
pinch of salt

Lightly oil a 20cm square dish.

Stir the sugar and honey together in a deep pot over a low heat until they have melted together, then add the lemon juice and water. Turn up the heat a little and simmer for 2–3 minutes, until you get a golden caramel. Turn off the heat, tip in the bicarbonate of soda and beat with a wooden spoon until it has all disappeared and the mixture is foaming. Scrape this into the dish immediately and leave to cool and set. This will take an hour or so.

If not using immediately, store in the freezer.

fried things

Sometimes a dish needs a fried thing; sometimes a fried thing needs a sauce. It's not always easy to tell, or remember, where a dish started – with the sauce or with the fried thing sitting on it.

fried artichokes

serves 4 as a snack or starter

2 lemons
4–8 young artichokes
plain flour seasoned with salt, for
    coating

Squeeze the juice of one lemon directly into a bowl of water and throw in the lemon halves too.

Trim the outer leaves of the artichokes to the paler yellowish flesh and snip off the top green parts. Peel the stem and base, also back to the paler flesh. Put the peeled artichokes into the acidulated water as you go to avoid discoloration.

Removing them one by one, cut each artichoke into thin slices lengthways, 2–3mm thick. You may get 3–6 slices per artichoke, depending on size. Put the slices back in the water.

Heat some oil in a deep-fryer to 180°C.

Drain the artichokes and toss them in the seasoned flour to coat lightly, shaking gently to remove the excess flour. Fry the slices in the hot oil until golden and crisp, then drain on kitchen paper. Season well with salt and drizzle with some lemon juice.

Serve as here with a drizzle of lemon juice and salt or with a sauce such as romesco (page 64).

The artichokes can be prepped and left in acidulated water an hour or two before frying.

cauliflower kofta

makes 20 small kofta

400g cauliflower florets (1 medium
    cauliflower)
40g gram flour
1 teaspoon ground turmeric
pinch of cayenne pepper

Roughly chop the cauliflower florets, then place in a food processor and pulse until the cauliflower is finely chopped. Place in a bowl with the gram flour, turmeric, cayenne and some salt and pepper and mix well.

You may need to add a little more gram flour, depending on the cauliflower. To test, gather some of the mixture in your hand and squeeze to see if it holds together. Form the mixture into balls, each weighing 20g.

Heat the oil in a deep-fryer to 180°C. Drop in a few of the cauliflower kofta and cook for 3–4 minutes, until brown and crisp. Serve immediately.

This will make 20 small kofta, enough to serve 4–6 people as the base of a main course, and it also works well as a snack. We use just one per portion in the beetroot rasam dish on page 54.

The kofta can be made and shaped ahead on the day and fried just before serving.

hazelnut & Templegall gougères

makes 12

Templegall is a mature Comté-style cheese made by Hegarty's in County Cork. It has the smooth, nutty flavour typical of the style and a lovely melting texture that works brilliantly in these fried gougères. A well-flavoured Cheddar would also be good. We serve these as a snack or as on page 40 with peperonata.

150g Templegall cheese
110g strong white flour
30g hazelnuts, roasted and finely
   chopped
170ml water
60g butter
2 medium eggs

Cut the cheese into 12 × 1cm cubes and grate the rest.
   Put the flour and hazelnuts in a food processor.
   Put the water and butter in a pan and bring to a boil.
   Start the food processor and pour in the hot water and butter, letting the motor run for 30 seconds to beat the liquid into the flour mix. Add one egg and beat until fully incorporated, then add the second egg and repeat. Finally, beat in the grated cheese and season with salt and pepper. Transfer the batter to a bowl and leave it in the fridge for at least 1 hour or up to overnight, until cool and firm.
   Wrap 1 tablespoon of the cooled batter around a cube of Templegall, shaping the gougère into a sphere. Repeat to make 12 gougères. Refrigerate until required.
   To serve, fry the gougères in vegetable oil at 180°C until crisp and fully cooked through.

The batter is best made the day before then filled on the day. The mixture also freezes well.

sesame gougères

makes 15–20

These came about when we wanted to put a gougère on the pumpkin seed mole on page 66 and our usual cheesy gougères were just too, well, cheesy. Having taken the cheese out, we went the whole hog and took the egg out too, making them vegan.

180ml water
2 tablespoons sesame oil
2 tablespoons nutritional yeast
1 tablespoon tahini
½ teaspoon salt
80g plain flour
½ teaspoon baking soda
90g sesame seeds
2 tablespoons aquafaba

Bring the water, oil, nutritional yeast, tahini and salt slowly to a boil in a pan, stirring. Whisk in the flour, then continue to stir over a low heat for 5–7 minutes, until the mixture becomes thick and doughy. Stir in the baking soda, sesame seeds and aquafaba and remove from the heat. Leave the mix to cool, then shape it into 20g balls and refrigerate or freeze until needed.
   To serve, fry the gougères in vegetable oil at 180°C until crisp and fully cooked through.

Can be made and shaped in advance and frozen or kept in the fridge overnight.

lemon arancini

makes 12–15

400ml vegetable stock
2 tablespoons olive oil
125g Carnaroli or other risotto rice
1 tablespoon white wine
zest and juice of 2 lemons
20g nutritional yeast
15g butter
panko breadcrumbs, to coat

Bring the stock to a boil, then reduce to a simmer to keep it hot over a low heat.

Heat the olive oil in a heavy-based frying pan over a low to medium heat. Add the rice and toast it, stirring, for 5–7 minutes. Add the white wine and half of the lemon zest and juice and simmer until absorbed. Add a ladle of stock and stir until it is absorbed, then add another and repeat until the rice is cooked through. Check often towards the end of the cooking – you may not need all of the stock.

Stir in the remaining lemon zest and juice along with the nutritional yeast and butter. Season well with salt and pepper.

Spread the risotto in a thin layer on a tray, cover with parchment and leave to cool. Once cooled, shape into balls approximately 40g each. Roll these in panko breadcrumbs to coat.

Refrigerate until required, then deep-fry for 4–5 minutes, until crisp and golden. Remove from the oil and drain on a tray lined with kitchen paper.

Makes 12–15 arancini, enough to serve 4–6 people as the base of a main course. The artichoke dish on page 16 uses just one per portion as a starter or small plate.

The risotto base can be made the day before and the arancini shaped on the day.

coriander panelle

makes approx. 36 slices

Panelle is classically a Sicilian street food snack, typically flavoured with parsley and served with a dusting of Pecorino and a generous squeeze of lemon juice. It's quite versatile, however, and works in many dishes the way fried polenta does. We use it as part of the summer bean and almond satay dish on page 68.

800ml water
250g gram flour
1 small bunch of fresh coriander, finely chopped
1 lemon

Bring the water to a boil in a pot, whisk in the gram flour and bring back to a boil. Reduce the heat to a low simmer and cook for 10–15 minutes, stirring all the time, until you have a smooth, thick paste. Add the chopped coriander and season generously with salt.

Transfer the paste to a loaf tin, level out the top and leave it to cool and set. Alternatively, spread the paste on a tray to a thickness of 1cm.

When the panelle has cooled, turn it out from the loaf tin and cut it into slices 1cm thick. Cut these slices again into two or three smaller rectangles or triangles.

To finish, deep-fry the panelle slices in hot oil until crisp on both sides. Drain on kitchen paper and drizzle generously with lemon juice.

The base can be made in advance and keeps for two or three days in the fridge but it's best to slice and fry just before serving.

pickles

This rapidly expanding corner of the storeroom is a fairly recent addition to the Paradiso repertoire, yet it's already hard to remember the time before pickles. They bring colour, crispness and, most usefully, a hit of vibrant acidity to any dish. Back in the day we tended to finish dishes with citrus, herbs and chillies, but now we are just as likely to say, 'What about a pickle?'

pickled beetroot

makes 1 large jar

3 medium beetroot
300ml white wine vinegar
150g caster sugar
1 tablespoon water
1 teaspoon salt

Peel and thinly slice the beetroot (approx. 2mm thick) using a mandolin or sharp knife.
   Bring the remaining ingredients to a boil in a small pot. Add the sliced beetroot and bring back to a boil. Remove from the heat and decant into a sterilised jar.

Keeps for at least three months if stored in the fridge after opening.

pickled red onion

makes 1 × 500g pickling jar

3 red onions, halved
100g caster sugar
200ml water
150ml apple cider vinegar
3 cloves
1 star anise
1 tablespoon salt

Cut the halved red onions lengthwise into slices 1cm thick. Put everything except the onions in a pot and bring to a boil, then add the onion slices and bring back to a boil. Remove from the heat and leave to cool in the liquid, then transfer into sterilised jars.

Keeps for at least three months if stored in a sterilised jar in the fridge after opening.

pickled red cabbage

makes 1 × 500g pickling jar

¼ head of red cabbage, halved
100g caster sugar
200ml water
150ml apple cider vinegar
3 cloves
1 star anise
1 tablespoon salt

Cut the halved red cabbage into slices 5mm thick and put them in a bowl. Put everything else in a pot and bring to a boil, then pour this over the cabbage. Leave to cool, then transfer into sterilised jars.

Keeps for at least three months if stored in a sterilised jar in the fridge after opening.

pickled jalapeño

makes 1 × 500g pickling jar

¼ medium carrot, peeled and
    thinly sliced
1 medium shallot, thickly sliced
2 garlic cloves, halved
2 sprigs of fresh thyme
2 sprigs of fresh rosemary
75g caster sugar
150ml white wine vinegar
150ml water
1 teaspoon salt
15 red jalapeño chillies, halved
    lengthways and deseeded

Put everything except the chillies in a
small pot and bring to a boil, then add
the halved chillies and bring back to a
boil. Remove from the heat and leave
to cool in the liquid, then transfer into
sterilised jars and store in the fridge.
To use, slice the long pieces into
half-moons.

Keeps for up to three months in the fridge.

The pickled jalapeños can be used as soon
as they have cooled but are best after at
least one day.

pickled orange

makes 1 large jar

This purée can be used as a chutney or
pickle or as the base for sauces, such as
the orange sauce with beetroot risotto
on page 12.

4 oranges, washed, deseeded and
    sliced into 5mm-thick rounds
350g caster sugar
300ml white wine vinegar
1 fresh hot red chilli, chopped
1 cinnamon stick
1 tablespoon fennel seeds

Simmer the orange slices in boiling
water for 30 minutes. Strain, discard the
water and put the orange slices back in
the pot with the rest of the ingredients.
Simmer for 30 minutes more. Leave to
cool, then store in a sterilised jar. Leave
for at least two days but preferably for
two weeks before using. The pickled
orange slices can be used whole,
chopped or as a purée.

To make a purée, blend the orange
slices in a food processor, adding a
little of the pickling liquid to get a thick
pouring consistency. Transfer this purée
to a sterilised jar.

Keeps for up to three months.

This pickle is ready to use after two days
but is best if left for at least two weeks.

pickled fennel

makes 1 large jar

2 medium fennel bulbs
1 tablespoon salt
1 litre warm water
50g caster sugar
150ml white wine vinegar
100ml water
½ orange, sliced

Trim the top and any tough outer leaves
from the fennel. Starting at the top, use
a mandoline to cut the bulb into thin
slices.

Dissolve the salt in the warm water,
add the sliced fennel and leave to soak
for 2 hours. Drain and discard the water.

Bring the sugar, vinegar and water to
a boil in a small pot. Add the drained
fennel and the orange slices. Bring back
to a boil, then decant immediately into
sterilised jars. Ensure that the fennel
is submerged in the liquid. Leave for
24 hours before using.

Keeps for up to three months in a
sterilised jar.

pickled radish

makes 6–10 portions

8–10 fresh radishes
60g caster sugar
125ml white wine vinegar
25ml water
1cm piece of fresh ginger, peeled
    and sliced
2 lime leaves
¼ tablespoon salt
½ teaspoon yellow mustard seeds

Trim the radishes, slice them into
3mm-thick rounds and place in a
heatproof bowl.
    Bring the rest of the ingredients to a
boil in a small pot and pour enough of
the hot liquid over the sliced radishes to
cover them. Leave for 5 minutes, then
remove the radishes from the liquid and
leave to cool to room temperature before
serving.

This is a quick pickle that needs to be used
the same day.

Used pickling liquid can be used once or
twice more.

pickled raisins

makes 1 × 500g pickling jar

250ml balsamic vinegar
125g caster sugar
250g raisins

Bring the balsamic vinegar and sugar to
a boil in a small pot, then add the raisins
and remove the pan from the heat.
Transfer the raisins to a sterilised jar and
leave to cool before storing in the liquid.

Keeps for up to three months.

The pickled raisins can be used as soon as
they have cooled but are best after at least
one day.

pickled plum & scorzonera

makes 6 portions

200ml rice wine vinegar
100g caster sugar
50ml water
1 star anise
1 strip of lemon peel
1 plum
½ thick scorzonera root

Put everything except the plum and scorzonera in a pot.

Cut the plum in half, then cut each half into thirds lengthways. Snip off the ends. Cut each lengthways piece into three horizontally to get wedges approx. 1cm thick. Place the plum pieces in a heatproof bowl.

Bring the pickling liquid to a boil in a small pot and pour some of it over the plum pieces, enough to cover them. Leave for 10 minutes.

Meanwhile, peel the scorzonera into thin slices (approx. 2mm) on a slight diagonal. Place these in a bowl of acidulated water.

After 10 minutes, strain the plums and set them aside to cool. Put the liquid back in the pot and bring it back to a boil.

Drain the scorzonera slices and rinse them briefly under cold water. Place them in a bowl and pour over the pickling liquid. Leave for 10 minutes, then strain.

The separate plum and scorzonera pickles are ready to use when cooled.

This is a fresh pickle that can be prepared quickly and needs to be used on the day.

Used pickling liquid can be used once or twice more.

pickled wild garlic buds

wild garlic flower buds
sherry vinegar to cover

Put the buds in a bowl, cover with sherry vinegar and leave for 30 minutes, then remove the pickled buds.

A quick pickle that needs to be used on the day.

The vinegar can be reused for pickling or put in a salad dressing.

sauces, ambient

If creating rich and complex dishes from plants is all about layering and building, then sauce is the first block after the foundation. There was a time when sauce almost exclusively meant a piping hot liquid poured over a dish. Now far more of our sauces are served at room temperature or just a little above it, in the form of purées, salsas and emulsions. Flavour is often more pronounced at a comfortable temperature and the diner has a little longer to savour the dish. Also, let's be honest – plating up is easier with an ambient sauce.

burnt aubergine purée

makes 6 portions

2 medium aubergines
4 cloves of roasted garlic (page 64)
2 tablespoons chopped fresh coriander
1 tablespoon light tahini
1 tablespoon olive oil
2 teaspoons lemon juice

Prick the whole aubergines with a fork and place them under a hot grill or on a barbecue. Cook for 20–30 minutes, turning them often, until the skin is blackened and the aubergines are very soft inside.

Cut the cooked aubergines in half lengthways and scoop out the flesh, discarding the skin. Put the flesh in a fine mesh colander for 10 minutes to drain away excess liquid.

Put the drained flesh in a food processor with the roasted garlic, chopped coriander, tahini, olive oil and lemon juice and purée to a smooth paste. Season with salt and check the texture and flavour. You may want to add a little more tahini, oil or lemon juice.

Can be made in advance and keeps for three or four days in the fridge.

cashew korma

makes 1 small jar (approx. 200g)

1 teaspoon cumin seeds
1 teaspoon fenugreek seeds
½ teaspoon caraway seeds
2 green cardamom pods
1 teaspoon cayenne pepper
½ teaspoon ground turmeric
150g cashew cheese (page 202)
juice of ½ lemon
25ml dan dan oil (page 195)

Toast and grind the seeds and cardamom pods very finely, then stir in the cayenne and turmeric. Whisk this into the cashew cheese along with the lemon juice and dan dan oil.

Can be made in advance and keeps for three or four days in the fridge.

courgette basil sauce

makes 4–6 portions

25g fresh basil leaves
250g courgette, weighed after deseeding
  (see the tip)
50g shallots, thinly sliced
1 small garlic clove, thinly sliced
25ml vegetable stock or water
25ml extra virgin olive oil

Blanch the basil and refresh by dropping
it into boiling water, then remove it
immediately to iced water and drain.
Place on kitchen paper to dry.
    Quarter the courgettes lengthways,
remove the seeds and slice the flesh
thinly.
    Heat a little olive oil in a pan over a
medium heat. Add the shallots, garlic
and courgettes and sauté together for
3–4 minutes, until lightly cooked. Cool
this mix rapidly by spreading it out flat
on a tray and placing it in the fridge.
    When cooled, put everything in a
blender and blend for 1–2 minutes to get
a smooth green purée. Pass through a
sieve and season with salt. Serve at room
temperature.

You will need two medium courgettes
to give the required weight of flesh after
deseeding.

This can be made in advance on the day
but it won't keep well overnight.

red cabbage sauce

makes 4–6 portions

½ red cabbage, juiced
1 red apple, juiced
1 small onion, chopped
2 garlic cloves
2 sprigs of fresh thyme
1 tablespoon sherry vinegar
100g unsalted butter, diced
¼ teaspoon xanthan gum

Put the cabbage and apple juices in a pot
with the onion, garlic and thyme. Bring
to a boil and simmer for 45 minutes.
Strain and return the liquid to the pot.
Add the sherry vinegar and whisk in
the butter to thicken slightly. Transfer
to a food processor and blend in the
xanthan gum. Leave to cool to room
temperature.

Can be made in advance and keeps for up
to a week in the fridge but bring it back to
room temperature before serving.

green herb sauce

makes 10 portions

200g cashew cheese (page 202)
20g fresh dill, chopped
20g fresh basil, chopped
20g fresh chives, chopped

Put the cheese in a high-powered food
processor and blend to get a smooth
purée. Add the chopped herbs and blend
again to get a smooth green purée.
Season with salt.

Keeps for one or two days in the fridge.

tarragon mustard sauce

makes 20 portions

200g cashew cheese (page 202)
40g fresh tarragon, chopped
20g Dijon mustard
20g fresh chives, chopped

Put the cheese in a high-powered food
processor and blend to get a smooth
purée. Add the mustard and chopped
herbs and blend again to get a smooth
green purée. Season with salt.

Keeps for one or two days in the fridge.

spiced carrot purée

makes 8 portions

1 red pepper
500g carrots, peeled and chopped
2 garlic cloves, peeled
30g harissa paste
100ml olive oil
1 tablespoon sherry vinegar
1 teaspoon cumin seeds, ground
½ teaspoon sweet smoked paprika
¼ teaspoon caraway seeds, ground

Roast the red pepper over a flame or under a grill until the skin is blackened all over. Place in a paper bag or in a tightly sealed bowl to cool and loosen the skin. When cool, peel and discard the skin and seeds. Weigh out 50g for this recipe.

Boil or steam the carrots until soft. Blanch the garlic by adding it to the water for 30 seconds at the end of the cooking time.

Strain the carrots and garlic and put them in a food processor with the rest of the ingredients. Blend to a smooth purée. Season well with salt and leave to cool.

Can be made in advance and keeps for three or four days in the fridge.

maple miso

makes 6–8 portions

2 tablespoons white miso
2 tablespoons maple syrup
2 tablespoons olive oil
1 tablespoon water

Whisk everything together to get a thick pouring consistency, adding a little more water if necessary.

This can be made up to a day in advance and keeps for two or three days in the fridge.

aubergine miso purée

makes 4–6 portions

1 aubergine
1 tablespoon miso
1 tablespoon sherry vinegar

Prick the whole aubergine with a fork and place it under a hot grill or on a barbecue. Cook for 20–30 minutes, turning often, until the skin is blackened and the aubergine is soft inside. Cut the cooked aubergine in half lengthways and scoop out the flesh, discarding the skin. Put the flesh in a fine sieve for 10 minutes to drain away any excess liquid, then put the aubergine flesh in a food processor with the miso, sherry vinegar and 1 tablespoon olive oil. Blend and season with salt.

This can be made up to a day in advance and keeps for two or three days in the fridge.

strange sauce

makes 350g

This is our version of the popular but weirdly named Sichuan 'strange sauce' or sometimes even 'strange flavour sauce'. It's great on noodles or greens and we use it to flavour a dipping sauce for the adzuki bean wontons on page 98.

75g black sesame seeds, lightly toasted
60g brown sugar
2 garlic cloves
1 tablespoon grated fresh ginger
100ml soy sauce
50ml dan dan oil (page 195)
50ml black Chinese vinegar (Chinkiang vinegar)

Put all the ingredients in a food processor and blend to a smooth paste.

Can be made well in advance and keeps for weeks in a jar in the fridge.

black sesame mayo

makes 220g

35ml aquafaba
2 teaspoons rice vinegar
6 cloves of roasted garlic (page 64)
125ml sunflower oil
50ml toasted sesame oil
1 tablespoon black sesame paste (see
  the tip)

Put the aquafaba, vinegar and roasted
garlic in a food processor. With the
motor running, drizzle in the sunflower
oil and then the toasted sesame oil until
everything is emulsified. Add the black
sesame paste and season with salt.

You can buy black sesame paste or make it
by grinding black sesame seeds in a high-
speed food processor.

Can be made in advance and keeps for
three or four days in the fridge.

miso mayo

makes 1 small jar

70ml aquafaba
2 tablespoons white miso
2 teaspoons mirin
2 teaspoons rice vinegar
¼ teaspoon xanthan gum
250ml sunflower oil

Put all the ingredients except the oil
in a jug or beaker suitable for a hand-
held blender. Use a hand-held blender
to bring everything together, then add
the oil in a slow trickle, blending all the
time, to get a mayonnaise consistency.
If the result is too thin, add a little more
oil; if it's too thick, blend in a little water.

Can be made in advance and keeps for
three or four days in the fridge.

caper dillisk aioli

makes 1 small jar

1 egg
juice of ½ lemon
1 tablespoon small capers, drained
  and rinsed
½ teaspoon dillisk powder
5 cloves of roasted garlic (page 64)
½ teaspoon Dijon mustard
125ml sunflower oil
2 tablespoons extra virgin olive oil

Put everything but the oils in a blender,
food processor or jug that fits a hand-
held blender. Combine the oils in a
separate jug.
　　Turn on the blender to a low speed
and slowly begin to drizzle in the mix
of the two oils, increasing the blending
speed after a while, until you get a thick
pouring emulsion.

Dillisk powder can be bought or made by
grinding dried dillisk in a spice grinder.

Can be made in advance and keeps for up
to a week in the fridge.

preserved lemon purée

makes 250ml

You can make your own preserved lemons by packing them whole in salt or chopping and layering them in salt, then waiting a month or more. We did this for a while but the first time we forgot to get ahead of ourselves, we gave it up and went back to buying good-quality jarred ones from Morocco.

We use big blobs and little dots of this to add colour and acidity to plates as well as using it to flavour aioli, mayonnaise, dressings and sauces.

150g preserved lemons
10g caster sugar
150ml olive oil

Coarsely chop the whole preserved lemons, discarding any seeds, then put in a blender with the sugar and oil. Blend to a smooth paste, adding a little water or preserving liquid if required. Store in a clean container or squeeze bottle in the fridge.

Keeps for a month in the fridge once opened.

preserved lemon & rosemary purée

makes 250ml

Make as for the preserved lemon purée but using a rosemary-infused oil. To infuse oil with rosemary, put 150ml olive oil in a small pan and add the leaves from three sprigs of rosemary. Heat the oil slowly until the leaves begin to dance gently, then remove from the heat and leave to infuse for at least 1 hour but preferably overnight. Strain off the leaves and keep the oil.

pepper harissa

makes 400ml (approx. 10–12 portions)

1 red pepper
250ml olive oil
100ml water
50g harissa paste

Roast the peppers under a hot grill until the skin is blackened and the peppers are soft. Place them in a tightly covered container for 20–30 minutes, until the peppers have cooled and the skin has loosened. Peel and discard the skin, stalk and seeds.

Chop the pepper flesh and place it in a pot with the oil and water. Bring to a boil and keep at a boil for 30 seconds.

Blend to a smooth emulsion in a blender or using a hand-held blender. Add the harissa paste and a pinch of salt. Leave to cool before serving.

Can be made in advance and keeps for up to a week in the fridge.

beetroot harissa

makes 500ml

200g roasted beetroot, peeled and
   chopped
250ml oil
100ml water
50g harissa paste

Put the chopped beetroot in a pot with
the oil and water. Bring to a boil and
keep at a boil for 30 seconds.
   Blend to a smooth emulsion in a
blender or with a hand-held blender.
Add the harissa paste and a pinch of salt
and blend again briefly. If necessary,
add a little water to get a thick pouring
consistency. Leave to cool before
serving.

Can be made in advance and keeps for up
to a week in the fridge.

coconut, cucumber & radish raita

makes 4–6 portions

¼ cucumber
40g thick coconut yogurt
4 small radishes, finely diced
6 fresh mint leaves, finely chopped
juice of ½ lime

Halve the cucumber, remove the seeds
and finely dice the flesh. Stir all the
ingredients together and season to taste.

This is best made just before serving so the
radish and cucumber flavours remain lively
and separate in the yogurt.

coriander yogurt

makes 10 portions

50g fresh coriander, chopped
200g yogurt (dairy or coconut)

Put the chopped coriander in a food
processor or blender with 2 tablespoons
of the yogurt. Blend to get a green liquid.
Remove to a bowl or jug and stir in the
remaining yogurt to get a thick pouring
consistency.

Can be made early on the day but doesn't
keep well overnight, as the coriander
discolours.

smoked tomato purée

makes 1 small jar

We get our smoked sun-dried tomatoes
from Olives West Cork.

200g smoked sun-dried tomatoes
200ml boiling water
50ml olive oil

Put the dried tomatoes in a bowl and
pour over the boiling water. Leave for
30 minutes to soften the tomatoes.
Add the olive oil and blend to a smooth
purée.

Keeps for weeks in a sealed container in
the fridge.

black garlic purée

makes 1 small jar

To make your own black garlic, set a
dehydrator to 60°C. Wrap some whole
garlic bulbs in tinfoil and leave them in
the dehydrator for three to four weeks,
turning once a week. Check each time
you turn them and leave until the cloves
are a rich black colour. Do we do that?
No. We buy black garlic from someone
with the time and space to have a
dehydrator full of garlic for weeks.

4 bulbs of black garlic
40ml lemon juice

Peel the black garlic and purée the cloves
and lemon juice in a food processor or
with a mortar and pestle. Season with
salt to taste.

Keeps for up to a week in the fridge.

black garlic salt

makes 100g

1 teaspoon black garlic purée (see above)
100g flaky sea salt

Gently rub the black garlic into the
salt until well combined. Spread this
on a dehydrator tray and dehydrate for
3 hours.

Keeps for two weeks in an airtight
container.

fennel caper salsa

makes 4 portions

1 fennel bulb
1 tablespoon olive oil
2 garlic cloves, thinly sliced
1 fresh green chilli, deseeded and
    thinly sliced
2 tablespoons small capers, rinsed
zest and juice of ½ lemon

Trim the fennel bulb, discarding any
tough outer leaves and saving the green
fronds. Cut the bulb into quarters,
cut out and discard the core and dice
the rest.
   Heat the olive oil in a pan and sauté
the fennel and garlic together for
2 minutes, until the fennel is translucent
but still firm. Add the chilli and capers
and remove the pan from the heat.
Transfer to a bowl and stir in the lemon
zest and juice. Check the seasoning and
add salt if required.

Can be made a few hours in advance but
doesn't keep well overnight.

sungold salsa

makes 6–8 portions

200g sungold tomatoes, halved
2 fresh red chillies, deseeded and sliced
2 tablespoons olive oil
1 tablespoon sherry vinegar

Put the halved sungolds in a small pan
with the chillies and olive oil. Let the
tomatoes simmer slowly over a low heat
for 2–3 minutes, until they are beginning
to soften. Off the heat, add the sherry
vinegar and a little salt.

Best made just before serving.

date jam

makes approx. 350g

300g tinned tomatoes (net drained
   weight)
90g dates, pitted and chopped
2 fresh mild red chillies, deseeded and
   chopped
120ml orange juice
45g caster sugar
2 tablespoons sherry vinegar
½ teaspoon sweet smoked paprika
½ teaspoon hot smoked paprika

Put the tomatoes, dates, chillies and
orange juice in a heavy-based pot and
bring to a boil, then reduce the heat
and simmer for 30 minutes, stirring
often. Add the sugar and sherry vinegar
and simmer for 5 minutes more. Add
the paprikas and simmer for 2 minutes
more. Season with salt. Blend to a
smooth paste with a hand-held blender
or in a food processor. Check the
seasoning and adjust as required.

Keeps for two or three weeks in a sealed
container in the fridge.

burnt orange sauce

makes 6 portions

2 whole blood oranges
500ml blood orange juice
300g caster sugar
2 teaspoons lemon juice

Score the whole blood oranges by
stabbing them with a small knife. To
reduce their bitterness, blanch them in
boiling water for 1 minute. Repeat this
four times, changing the water each
time. Boil them again for 1 hour or so,
until soft.

At the same time, reduce the blood
orange juice to 300ml in a pan over a
low heat.

Using half the sugar (150g) and
1 teaspoon of the lemon juice, make a
dark caramel by cooking them slowly
over a low heat. Add the softened whole
blood oranges, breaking them up a little
in the pot with a wooden spoon, and
cook until the liquid is almost gone.
Add the reduced blood orange juice and
reduce again by half. Set aside.

Make a second dark caramel with the
remaining 150g sugar and the remaining
teaspoon of lemon juice. Put both
caramels in a blender and blend to a
smooth sauce.

Keeps for a week in the fridge.

sauces, hot

Hot as in temperature, that is – good old-fashioned broths and gravies that deliver warm, comforting blankets of flavour.

beetroot port gravy

makes 6–8 portions

Make beetroot juice by juicing beetroot or, next best thing, by blending and straining cooked beetroot through a fine sieve. Store-bought isn't as good as either of these – believe me, we tried one time when the juicer packed up.

400ml beetroot juice
200ml port
200ml tomato passata
1 small red onion, finely chopped
1 stick of celery or small piece of
    celeriac, diced
2 garlic cloves, chopped
1 whole clove
80g cold unsalted butter, diced

Put all the ingredients except the butter in a pot, bring to a boil and simmer for 20 minutes. Blend to a purée and push through a fine sieve to get a clear but slightly thickened liquid.
    Return this to the hob in a clean pot and simmer to reduce to half the volume. Set aside until serving if making ahead.
    Just before serving, bring the beet stock to a boil and gradually whisk in the cubes of cold unsalted butter to get a smooth, thickened gravy.

Can be made the day before but is best made early on in the day and set aside to be finished when serving.

miso gravy

serves 4

40g miso
40g unsalted butter, softened
50ml vegetable stock or water
1 teaspoon sherry vinegar

Whisk the miso and butter together until fully combined. Put this in a pan, add the stock or water and the sherry vinegar and slowly bring up to a simmer, whisking all the time, to get a smooth pouring gravy consistency.

The miso and butter mix can be made in advance and keeps for a week in the fridge.

nettle broth

makes 4 portions

80g nettle leaves (use only young nettle
    leaves from the top of the plant)
75ml olive oil
50g shallots, thinly sliced
1 garlic clove, thinly sliced
180ml vegetable stock

Bring a pot of salted water to a boil. Add the nettle leaves and leave for 1 minute before removing and refreshing them in cold water. Strain and leave the blanched nettles to dry for a few minutes.
    Using a little of the olive oil, sauté the shallots and garlic in a small pan for 4–5 minutes, until translucent. Remove from the pan and leave to cool.
    Put the blanched nettles, the cooked shallots and garlic, the rest of the olive

oil and the stock in a blender and blend to a smooth purée. Pass this through a fine sieve and season with salt. Reheat gently to serve.

Best made on the day but will keep overnight.

wild garlic broth

serves 4

75ml olive oil
75g shallots, finely chopped
50g wild garlic leaves
180ml vegetable stock or water

Heat a little of the oil in a pan and gently soften the shallots without colouring them, then leave to cool.

Blanch the wild garlic in boiling water for 20 seconds, then transfer to ice-cold water to stop the cooking and retain the colour. Pour the water off through a colander and leave the wild garlic to dry for a few minutes.

Blend the shallots, wild garlic and the stock or water together in a food processor, pass through a fine sieve and season with salt. Reheat gently to serve.

Best made on the day but will keep overnight.

coconut tamarind broth

serves 4 or 8

This serves 4 for the tofu, aubergine and napa cabbage curry on page 162 or serves 8 as the sauce for the chilli-glazed tofu on page 84.

80g fresh ginger, peeled and thickly
   sliced
50g shallots, peeled and halved
40g carrot, peeled and coarsely chopped
1–2 fresh red chillies, coarsely chopped
2 garlic cloves
50g coconut cream

1 × 400ml tin of coconut milk
150ml vegetable stock or water
2 dried lime leaves
1 small bunch of fresh coriander
1 small bunch of fresh basil
1 teaspoon tamarind concentrate
¼ teaspoon ground turmeric

Put the ginger, shallots, carrot, chillies and garlic in a food processor and pulse to a finely minced texture.

Heat a little oil in a pot, then add the vegetable mix and sauté for 3–4 minutes. Add the coconut cream, coconut milk, stock or water, dried lime leaves and fresh herbs. Bring to a boil, then simmer over a low heat for 30 minutes, stirring occasionally. Pass through a fine sieve, saving the liquid and discarding the solids.

Add the tamarind concentrate and turmeric to the broth and season well with salt.

Can be made the day before but is best made early on the day.

walnut miso sauce

serves 4

1 garlic clove, crushed
50ml olive oil
2 tablespoons miso
100ml water
150g walnuts
1 teaspoon sherry vinegar
pinch of cayenne pepper

Sauté the garlic in a little of the olive oil in a small pan for 1 minute. Add the miso, then whisk in the water to get a smooth paste. Put this in a food processor with the walnuts, sherry vinegar and the remaining olive oil and blend to a smooth purée. Season carefully with salt and a pinch of cayenne pepper. Reheat gently to serve.

Can be made in advance and keeps for two or three days in the fridge.

lemon ginger beurre blanc

serves 4–6

zest of 1 lemon
30ml lemon juice
25ml white wine
50g grated fresh ginger, squeezed to
    separate the juice
15g sliced shallot
4 black peppercorns
2 tablespoons cream
200g unsalted butter, cut into
    small cubes

Combine the lemon zest and juice, white wine, grated ginger, shallot and peppercorns in a heavy-based saucepan and simmer to reduce by half. Add the cream and bring back to a simmer, then slowly whisk in the cold butter cubes one at a time until emulsified. Whisk in the ginger juice and season with salt.

Use immediately or keep warm to avoid it splitting. If reheating, start with a dash of cream in a small pan and whisk in 1 tablespoon of the beurre blanc at a time.

This doesn't keep and must be made just before serving.

ginger lime curry

serves 6

1 small carrot
2 shallots
3 garlic cloves
15g fresh coriander
15g fresh parsley
1 lemongrass stalk
80g fresh ginger, grated
1 tablespoon jerk spice (page 201)
300ml coconut milk
250ml tomato passata
15g light brown sugar
zest and juice of 2 limes

Peel and roughly chop the carrot, shallots and garlic. Roughly chop the fresh coriander and parsley. Place them all in a food processor and blitz until very finely chopped.

Bruise the lemongrass with the back of a knife or a rolling pin.

Heat a little oil in a pan over a medium heat. Add the finely chopped vegetables and the lemongrass and sauté for 5 minutes. Add the grated ginger and jerk spice and cook for 1 minute more. Add the coconut milk, passata, brown sugar and lime zest. Bring to a boil, then simmer over a low heat for 30 minutes. Pass the sauce through a fine sieve.

Stir in the lime juice and season with salt.

Can be made in advance and keeps for three or four days in the fridge.

sweetcorn espuma

makes 1 siphon of espuma

250g sweetcorn kernels
25g onion, finely chopped
100ml water
75ml cream

Place the sweetcorn, onion and water in a small saucepan and simmer for 2 minutes. Blend for 2 minutes, then push through a fine sieve, retaining the liquid and discarding the solids. Season with salt. Put 125ml of the liquid in a siphon with the 75ml of cream and charge with gas (or see the tip).

This makes enough for double the cappelloni recipe on page 46.

This requires a foaming siphon. Without one, the best option is to blend the ingredients with a hand-held blender to get a light purée.

dressings, oils & butters

Dressings and oils bring complexity to cooked and raw vegetables, sometimes on the plate but more often in the pan just at the end of cooking. We use butters to envelop pasta, gnocchi and bakes with richness and lively flavours.

maple sesame ginger dressing

makes 100ml (6–8 portions)

20g finely grated fresh ginger
30ml rice vinegar
25ml tamari
20ml sesame oil
15ml maple syrup

Whisk everything together. Store in a jar and shake well before use.

Keeps well in the fridge for a week.

psb dressing

makes 100ml (6–8 portions)

This was first made for a purple sprouting broccoli dish, hence the abbreviation psb. It's now used for most green things and is usually added to the pan at the end of cooking.

1 small garlic clove, grated
45ml tamari or soy sauce
1 tablespoon grated fresh ginger
2 teaspoons toasted sesame oil
2 teaspoons mirin

Whisk everything together. Store in a jar and shake well before use.

Keeps for up to a week in the fridge.

shallot dressing

makes 150ml (10–12 portions)

This is practically the house dressing, the one we reach for most often to flavour an element of a dish.

40g shallot, very finely diced
½ teaspoon salt
60ml sherry vinegar
60ml extra virgin olive oil

Put the shallot and salt into a jar and leave for 1 minute. Add the sherry vinegar, olive oil and some black pepper and shake to combine.

Keeps for up to a week in the fridge.

mustard vinaigrette

makes 180ml (12–15 portions)

50ml soy sauce
2 tablespoons wholegrain mustard
4 small pickled silverskin onions, very
   finely chopped
100ml olive oil

Put all the ingredients in a jar and shake for a few seconds to combine.

Keeps for up to a week in the fridge.

hazelnut rayu

makes 250ml (approx. 15 portions)

125ml vegetable oil
3 garlic cloves, finely minced
25g fresh ginger, peeled and finely
    minced
1 spring onion, finely chopped
75g hazelnuts, toasted and coarsely
    chopped
15g sesame seeds, lightly toasted
40ml sesame oil
1 tablespoon soy sauce
1 tablespoon Korean hot pepper flakes

Warm the vegetable oil in a saucepan over a low heat. Add the garlic, ginger and spring onion and cook for a few minutes, until the garlic just starts to colour. Add the rest of the ingredients and take the pan off the heat. Season with a little salt. Leave to cool, then store in a jar or airtight container.

Keeps for up to a week in the fridge.

black garlic peanut rayu

makes 350ml (approx. 20 portions)

100ml sunflower oil
3 garlic cloves, sliced
1½ tablespoons Korean hot
    pepper flakes
8 black garlic cloves
40g grated fresh ginger
100g peanuts, toasted and coarsely
    chopped
3 spring onions, finely sliced
15g toasted sesame seeds
70ml tamari
50ml toasted sesame oil
30ml maple syrup

Put the sunflower oil, sliced garlic and Korean hot pepper flakes in a heavy-based pan. Bring to a simmer, then cook over a low heat until the garlic is just beginning to colour. Strain through a fine sieve, keeping the oil and garlic separate.

Add the black garlic cloves and ginger to the strained oil and blend to a smooth purée. Stir all the remaining ingredients into the purée, including the cooked garlic and hot pepper flakes.

Keeps for weeks in the fridge.

chermoula

makes 180ml (8–10 portions)

½ teaspoon cumin seeds, lightly toasted
½ teaspoon fennel seeds
25g fresh coriander
40g fresh parsley
10g fresh mint
1 garlic clove, chopped
zest of ½ lemon
zest of ½ orange
pinch of cayenne pepper
125ml olive oil

Grind the cumin and fennel seeds in a pestle and mortar. Add the rest of the ingredients except the oil and grind to a fine paste. Transfer to a container and add the oil. Season with salt.

Keeps for three or four days in a sealed jar in the fridge but is best made within 24 hours of using, as the flavours tend to muddle over time.

If using a food processor instead of a pestle and mortar, you may need to double the quantities. Made this way, it keeps for a week or so.

chimichurri

makes 200ml (10–12 portions)

50g fresh parsley, finely chopped
25g fresh oregano, finely chopped
1 fresh red chilli, finely chopped
1 garlic clove, crushed
100ml extra virgin olive oil
2 tablespoons sherry vinegar
¼ teaspoon freshly ground black pepper

Mix all the ingredients together and season with salt.

Keeps for two or three days in the fridge.

zhoug

makes 200ml (10–12 portions)

110g fresh red chillies, deseeded and
   chopped
40g fresh coriander, chopped
1 garlic clove, chopped
4 cardamom seeds, ground
150ml extra virgin olive oil

Put the chillies, fresh coriander, garlic and ground cardamom in a food processor and blend to a finely minced texture. Add the oil and a little salt and pulse a couple times to mix without fully emulsifying. The texture of this zhoug is very finely chopped to give a green and red flecked sauce/dressing. Blending it further can result in a purée that easily turns brown. Taste and add more salt if required.

Keeps for two days in the fridge.

dan dan oil

makes 1 litre

This is a very hot oil with layers of fragrance from the star anise and cinnamon.

60g Sichuan peppercorns, coarsely
   chopped
20g dried bird's eye chillies, coarsely
   chopped
20g Korean hot pepper flakes
6 star anise
2 cinnamon sticks, broken
1 litre sunflower oil

Put everything in a saucepan and heat gently on a very low heat until the oil is just beginning to simmer. Turn off the heat, cover the pan with a lid and leave to stand for at least 1 hour, but preferably for up to 24 hours.
   Pass through a fine sieve (and, if necessary, a piece of kitchen paper) to get a clear oil. Discard the solids and store the oil.

Keeps well for up to three months.

lovage oil

makes 125ml

50g lovage leaves
125ml sunflower oil

Blanch the lovage leaves by dropping them into boiling water, then removing immediately to a bowl of cold water. Squeeze out the water and roughly chop the blanched leaves.
   Blend the leaves with the oil to get a smooth green oil. Strain through a fine sieve and muslin overnight.

Keeps for two to three weeks in a sealed bottle or jar.

basil oil

makes 200ml

100g fresh basil
200ml olive oil

Blanch the basil in boiling water for a few seconds, then immediately remove it and cool it in iced water. Leave on kitchen paper to dry, then blend with the olive oil. Leave for 1 hour before straining out the solids.

Keeps for three or four days.

For coriander oil, simply replace the basil with fresh coriander and proceed as above.

vanilla oil

makes 250ml

250ml sunflower oil
1 vanilla bean

Warm the oil to 60°C. Split the vanilla bean in half lengthways and scrape the seeds into the warm oil. Transfer the oil to a sterilised bottle or jar and add the whole vanilla bean. Leave for 12 hours before using, shaking occasionally to help the flavour extraction.

Keeps for at least three weeks.

sungold butter

serves 6–8

Great with pasta or for breakfast as a substitute for hollandaise.

500g sungold tomatoes
100–120g butter

Put the sungolds in a small pot and break them up with your hands or a potato masher. Bring to a boil and keep at a high simmer for 30 minutes. Blend coarsely with a hand-held blender, then pass it through a fine sieve. Add half the sungolds' weight of butter and blend again. Season with salt. Set aside and reheat gently to use.

Keeps for a week in the fridge.

sage & chilli butter

makes 150g (8–10 portions as a pasta butter)

Korean chilli flakes give this butter a great colour and a mild chilli hit. For a stronger spicing, use ground bird's eye chillies.

8 fresh sage leaves, finely chopped
1 tablespoon Korean hot pepper flakes
150g butter, softened
1 teaspoon lemon juice
zest of 1 orange

Stir the chopped sage leaves and Korean chilli flakes into the softened butter, then beat in the lemon juice and orange zest.

Keeps for a week or more in the fridge and freezes well.

orange butter

makes 60g (4–6 portions as a pasta butter)

zest and juice of ½ orange
1 teaspoon lemon juice
60g unsalted butter, softened

Reduce the citrus juices to 1 tablespoon in a small pot over a low heat, then stir this syrup and the orange zest into the softened butter with a pinch of salt.

Keeps for up to a week in the fridge and freezes well.

saffron hazelnut butter

makes 6–8 portions

40g hazelnuts
40ml orange juice
large pinch of saffron threads
zest of 1 orange
150g unsalted butter, diced and softened
    a little

Preheat the oven to 150°C fan.

Roast the hazelnuts on a tray for 20–30 minutes, until the skins are blistering. Wrap the warm nuts in a clean tea towel and leave to steam for 1 minute, then rub the loose skins off, ignoring any that remain attached. Chop the hazelnuts coarsely with a knife or by breaking them with a rolling pin.

Bring the orange juice and saffron to a boil, then simmer until syrupy. Add the orange zest and remove the pan from the heat.

Put the softened butter in a bowl and mix in the rest of the ingredients along with a pinch of salt. Wrap the finished butter into a log in parchment paper and store in the fridge or freezer until required.

Can be made in advance. Keeps well for a week in the fridge and a month or more in the freezer.

jalapeño butter

makes 250g

We sometimes make a red version as well and use both together.

15 green jalapeños
225g unsalted butter, diced
¼ teaspoon xanthan gum

Juice the jalapeños. Bring the juice to a boil, then transfer to a blender with the butter and xanthan gum. Blend until smooth and season with salt.

Can be made in advance. Keeps for two days in the fridge.

This makes enough for double the cappelloni recipe on page 46, but it's hard to make a smaller amount given the need to juice the peppers.

lime butter

makes 180g (10–12 portions as a pasta butter)

zest and juice of 2 limes
180g unsalted butter, softened

Put the lime zest and juice in a small pan and reduce by half, then stir into the butter with a pinch of salt.

Keeps for a week or more in the fridge and freezes well.

For lemon butter, simply replace the lime with lemon.

pulses

During the first few years of Paradiso, there was neither sight nor sound of a bean or a lentil on the menus. Not because I didn't like beans and lentils, but because they had come to stand for something I was trying to get away from.

Vegetarian restaurants at the time were symbiotic with the health food industry, to the extent that it seemed unlikely that one even existed outside of that relationship or would be able to breathe for itself. Vegetarianism – an ethical principle – had been subsumed into a vague concept of being careful about what you put in your precious and delicate body. Vegetarian food sold itself as healthy first and tasty second, or third, or worse. People who wanted to avoid all sorts of things in their diet – wheat, sugar, fat, etc. – went to vegetarian restaurants and expected to be fed there. The vegetarian restaurants complied because, well, they were mostly inside health food shops.

I wanted to make food that was bright and loud and full of pleasurable flavour, and Paradiso was to be a place where I would be free to do that. I didn't really have much detail on how I was going to go about it, but it turned out that banning pulses (and rice!) from the kitchen was a great place to start. Without your familiars, you have to find a new way to work, right? I needed people to easily understand that Paradiso was not your ordinary vegetarian restaurant. How to do that? Well, big, loud flavours, colourful food, loads of spice, herbs, cheese ... and no pulses.

In time, once I felt secure and confident in what I was doing, I let them in. Puy and beluga lentils have become an important part of our repertoire and to a lesser extent, chickpeas, just because they are so versatile. We use broad beans all year round, freezing much of the crop from Gortnanain so that we always have some to hand. There are no recipes for broad beans in the book. We boil them, peel them and scatter them on loads of dishes whenever a bright finish of freshness and colour is called for. Similarly, Gortnanain produces a hefty crop of borlotti every year and most of those go in the freezer too, to be used through the winter and as far into the spring as the stock lasts. Sometimes they meet the next crop coming round again. Happy days.

Here, then, are just two recipes for our favourite pulse dishes.

braised beluga lentils

serves 4 as a main or 8–10 as part of another dish

1 litre vegetable stock or water
1 medium shallot, finely chopped
1 garlic clove, finely chopped
40ml red wine
250g beluga lentils
3 sprigs of fresh thyme

Bring the stock or water to a boil and keep it on a low simmer.

Sauté the shallot in a little olive oil over a medium heat for 2 minutes. Add the garlic and continue to cook for a few minutes more, until slightly golden.

Add the wine and bring to a boil, then reduce until it's almost evaporated. Add the beluga lentils and thyme sprigs.

Pour in half of the hot stock or water, reduce the heat and simmer until the liquid is almost gone.

Add half of the remaining stock or water and simmer again until the liquid is almost gone again. Check the lentils – they should be perfectly done with just a little bite of texture. If not, add a little more liquid at a time until they are done. The total cooking time should be 20–25 minutes. Season with salt and black pepper.

Can be made up to a day ahead. Keeps for two or three days in the fridge.

The lentils will serve 8–10 as a small element of a dish such as the aubergine parcels on page 52, where only 1–2 tablespoons is a portion, or are enough to make four substantial bowls such as the staff dinner on page 150.

lemon braised borlotti

makes 4–8 portions

400g fresh borlotti beans, weighed after
   shelling
120ml olive oil
4 garlic cloves, finely chopped
1 tablespoon fresh thyme leaves
zest and juice of 2 lemons

Put the beans in a pot and cover generously with cold water. Bring to a boil, then reduce the heat and simmer gently for 10 minutes. Check the beans and cook for a further 5–10 minutes, until the beans have the texture of just tender potato. Drain.

Put the oil in the pot with the garlic and thyme leaves and simmer for 1 minute, then add the warm beans and the lemon zest and juice. Season well with salt and black pepper. Turn off the heat, cover the pot and leave to marinate for at least 30 minutes. Warm gently before serving.

Can be made up to two days in advance. Keeps for four or five days in the fridge.

spice mixes

When a dish has a long list of ingredients to be put together every day or two, it makes sense to shorten the prep time by having the basic spice mix to hand. It's also easier to make spice mixes in larger quantities rather than doing complicated maths like dividing teaspoons by three and testing the patience of a weighing scales.

These are some of the mixes that we make once a fortnight or so during the time their dish is on the menu.

couscous spice

makes approx. 120g

2 tablespoons cumin seeds
2 tablespoons fennel seeds
1 tablespoon coriander seeds
½ teaspoon caraway seeds
1 tablespoon ground turmeric
1 teaspoon sweet smoked paprika
½ teaspoon salt

Toast the seeds and leave to cool for a few minutes, then grind them together. Stir in the turmeric, paprika and salt. Store in a dry airtight container.

Keeps well for two weeks.

Makes enough for four batches of the couscous cake on page 82.

smoky za'atar

makes approx. 100g

1 tablespoon cumin seeds
1 tablespoon coriander seeds
1 tablespoon fresh thyme leaves
1 tablespoon sesame seeds, toasted
1 tablespoon sumac
1 tablespoon hot smoked paprika
½ teaspoon salt

Toast the cumin and coriander seeds and leave to cool for a few minutes, then grind them together with the thyme. Stir in the toasted sesame seeds, sumac, paprika and salt. Store in a dry airtight container.

Keeps well for two weeks.

togarashi

makes 200g

45g Szechuan peppercorns
45g black sesame seeds
35g white sesame seeds
3 nori sheets
8g dried bird's eye chillies
30g dried orange rind
40g poppy seeds

Separately, toast the Szechuan peppercorns, the black and white sesame seeds and the nori sheets.

Grind the toasted peppercorns and nori with the chillies and orange rind in a spice grinder. Add the sesame and poppy seeds to the ground mix and pulse once or twice to combine.

Keeps well for two weeks or more.

To make togarashi oil, put 2 tablespoons of togarashi and 200ml of sesame oil in a small pan. Slowly bring to a simmer, then remove the pan from the heat and leave to infuse for at least 1 hour. Strain out and discard the solids.

jerk spice

makes 60g

15 dried bird's eye chillies
2 cinnamon sticks, broken
4 teaspoons black peppercorns
1 teaspoon cumin seeds, lightly toasted
2 teaspoons fresh thyme leaves
2 teaspoons allspice
1 teaspoon grated nutmeg
1 teaspoon smoked paprika
¼ teaspoon cayenne pepper

Grind together the chillies, cinnamon sticks, peppercorns and cumin seeds. Add the thyme leaves and pulse briefly to chop them into the mix. Transfer the mix to a bowl and stir in the remaining ingredients. Store in a dry airtight container.

Keeps well for two weeks or more.

This makes enough for four batches of the ginger lime curry on page 192.

ras el hanout

makes 50g

There is no definitive blend for this spice mix, which translates along the lines of 'top of the shelf', suggesting that every shop and every home might well have its own recipe. Ours varies from time to time, but this is a fairly typical blend.

10 black peppercorns
4 cloves
1 teaspoon cumin seeds
1 teaspoon coriander seeds
10 cardamom pods, seeds only
4 dried rose bud petals
1 teaspoon ground ginger
1 teaspoon ground mace
1 teaspoon ground nutmeg
1 teaspoon ground cinnamon
1 teaspoon ground allspice
1 teaspoon ground turmeric

Grind the peppercorns, cloves, cumin, coriander and cardamom finely. Separately, grind the rose bud petals coarsely. Combine all the ingredients and store in a dry airtight container.

Keeps well for two weeks or more.

dairy alternatives

We strive to make our vegan menu as close as possible to the one with dairy elements. Sometimes this involves making a totally different dish with the main vegetable ingredients, while other times we replace the cheese with a vegan alternative. Here are recipes for two vegan cheeses that we make and that successfully substitute for soft cheeses in dishes like the aubergine parcels on page 52. There is also a sweet version that whips up nicely for desserts. And there's a recipe for a vegan butter that works in all the places dairy butter does.

cashew cheese

makes 500g

300g cashews
20g garlic, sliced
50g shallots (optional)
15g salt
165ml filtered water
120ml lemon juice

Boil the cashews and garlic in water for 10 minutes. Strain and rinse well.

Put the cashews and garlic in a food processor with the shallots (if using), salt, filtered water and lemon juice. Blend for 2–3 minutes to get a smooth purée.

Keeps well in the fridge for up to a week.

The shallots add a savoury flavour but you can make it without them.

almond feta

makes 275g

200g flaked almonds
150ml water
2 garlic cloves
2 teaspoons salt
juice of 1 lemon
75ml olive oil

Preheat the oven to 180°C fan.

Boil the flaked almonds for 10 minutes in the water, then strain and rinse. Blend the rinsed almonds with the rest of the ingredients until very smooth.

Pour the mix into a small parchment-lined dish and bake in the oven for 40 minutes. Remove from the oven and leave to cool and set. When fully cooled, store the cheese in an airtight container in the fridge.

Keeps for up to a week in the fridge.

sweet almond cream

makes approx. 300g

200g flaked almonds
150ml water
100g caster sugar
juice of 1 lemon
75ml sunflower oil
1 teaspoon vanilla extract

Preheat the oven to 180°C fan.

Boil the flaked almonds for 10 minutes in the water, then strain and rinse. Blend the rinsed almonds with the rest of the ingredients until very smooth.

Pour the mix into a small parchment-lined dish and bake in the oven for 40 minutes. Remove from the oven and leave to cool and set. When fully cooled, store in an airtight container for up to a week.

To serve, whip some of the set cream with a whisk, adding a little almond milk if required to get a soft whipped consistency.

Keeps for up to a week in the fridge.

vegan butter

makes 275g

50ml soya milk
2 teaspoons white wine vinegar
200ml refined, unscented coconut oil
1 tablespoon sunflower oil
⅛ teaspoon xanthan gum
pinch of ground turmeric

Whisk the soya milk and vinegar together and leave it for 5 minutes. Gently melt the coconut oil.

Blend everything in a food processor, then transfer to a container and refrigerate to set.

Keeps well in the fridge for a week or more.

index

acknowledgements

Thanks to Kristin Jensen of Nine Bean Rows for the way she guided this project with such seemingly effortless skill, care and attention to detail. I might have been intimidated if I had known how brilliant she is when sending a cold call email wondering if she'd be interested in working together.

It was fantastic to have John Foley of Bite Design back on board, having previously worked with him on my first two books. John's contribution is always so much more than a credit for design and layout suggests. He creates an essence of the end product early on, making something tangible for others to work inside.

Thanks, too, to photographer Ruth Calder-Potts and to food stylist Charlotte O'Connell for bringing their own strong styles to the look and feel of the book. Those photo shoot days felt like the very best kind of creative teamwork.

The recipes in this book are not all mine. Even those that are have evolved in the constant reworking of a repertoire that is the day-to-day business of a creative kitchen. Special thanks must go to Eneko Lopez, head chef from 2017 to 2019, who was the first to bring his own creative identity to the kitchen and who quietly taught me to let go and learn the art of collaboration. Thanks also to Meadhbh Halton, head chef from 2020 to 2022, who steered us through topsy-turvy times and who put a lot of the early spadework into this book. Miguel Frutos was barely in the door as head chef as we wrapped up this book, but he quickly added a few recipes and we are excited to have him on board.

A restaurant is more than a parade of head chefs, of course, and one that is thirty years on the go is made up of more people than could be named on one sheet of paper. Literally hundreds of people have kept Paradiso paddling along over the years and it is a testament to all of them that I seem to say every year or so that this is the best Paradiso yet. Special thanks to those who have been here for the long haul, connecting the past, present and future: Dave O'Mahony, Ro Romero and Glory Mongin; to the current crew (the best ever, obviously); and to those yet to come.

And finally, a personal indulgence – thanks always to and for Maureen.

about the author

Denis Cotter is the owner and executive chef of Paradiso in Cork, where his inventive and flavour-driven food has been at the forefront of vegetable cuisine since the restaurant opened in 1993.

He is the author of four previous books: *The Café Paradiso Cookbook* (1999), *Paradiso Seasons* (2003), *Wild Garlic, Gooseberries ... and Me* (2007) and *For the Love of Food* (2011). Denis is always working and yet always trying to retire to pursue his other career as a barman and to find the time to learn to play trombone.

NINE
BEAN
ROWS

Nine Bean Rows
23 Mountjoy Square
Dublin
D01 E0F8
Ireland
@9beanrowsbooks
ninebeanrowsbooks.com

First published 2023
© Denis Cotter, 2023

ISBN: 978-1-7392105-0-2

Recipes by Denis Cotter, Meadhbh Halton, Eneko Lopez and Miguel Frutos
Editor: Kristin Jensen
Design and layout: John Foley bitedesign.com
Food photography: Ruth Calder-Potts ruthcalderpotts.com
Food styling: Charlotte O'Connell charlotteoconnell.co.uk
Proofreader: Annie Lee
Printed by L&C Printing Group, Poland

The paper in this book is produced using pulp from managed forests.

10 9 8 7 6 5 4 3 2 1